Data Privacy Law:
A Practical Guide

2nd Edition

G.E. Kennedy & L.S.P. Prabhu

ISBN: 978-0-9995127-1-5

TABLE OF CONTENTS

PREFACE   i

CONTENT OVERVIEW   iii

ABOUT THE AUTHORS   iv

CHAPTER ONE – Who Needs a Data Privacy Policy?   1

    A. Introduction   1

    B. What is the Difference Between Data Privacy and Data Security?   3

    C. Why Do Businesses Collect Personal Information?   5

    D. Is the Need for a Data Privacy Policy Urgent?   8

    E. Use of Third-Party Vendors   13

    F. Who's in Charge?   16

CHAPTER TWO – Compliance with Data Privacy Laws: A Survey of U.S. and Canadian Law and Multijurisdictional Conflicts   19

    A. Introduction   19

    B. United States Data Privacy Laws   20

    C. Canadian Data Privacy Laws   29

CHAPTER THREE – EU Data Protection Legislation   45

A. Introduction   45

B. The Directives   47

C. The EU Data Protection Directive Governing   49
Principles

D. Examples of Data Protection Legislation   58
Enacted Based on the Data Protection
Directive's Principles

E. Does Having a Data Protection Officer Help   61
with Compliance?

CHAPTER FOUR – Regional Trends and   64
Multijurisdictional Conflicts

A. Regional Trends   64

B. Multijurisdictional Conflicts in Data Privacy   74
Laws

CHAPTER FIVE – Outsourcing   80

A. Introduction   80

B. Use of a Cloud Service Provider to Collect,   81
Store and Transfer Information

C. Data Breach Insurance   83

CHAPTER SIX – Responding to an Incident   85

A. Incidence Response Timing and Process   85

B. Training   96

C. Data Retention and Disposal   99

D. Enforcement Actions   104

CHAPTER SEVEN – The Data Privacy Policy   109

A. Introduction   109

B. What Should Be Included in a Data Privacy Policy?   110

C. Data Classification   111

D. Collecting and Processing Personal Information   115

E. Required Provisions   118

SAMPLE PRIVACY POLICY TEMPLATE   124

HOW TO KEEP UPDATED   127

APPENDIX – Multijurisdictional Data Privacy Matrix   131

PREFACE

The Internet has greatly leveled the playing field by enabling smaller companies to enter international commerce. However, it has not simplified the underlying laws and regulations which govern international trade and data exchange. The ease of selling to foreign buyers has thus created a gap in awareness of international data privacy law, which is why this book is needed.

Our objective is to provide non-specialists with a sound understanding of the legal environment surrounding international e-commerce as it relates to data privacy. Above all, it is intended to be a practical guide which gives readers actionable advice.

While strict data privacy rules are rapidly becoming universal requirements, we would also like to stress the positive impact they have on a company's governance and sustainability of business practices. This is a key area which investors examine when determining a business' readiness to scale.

The laws governing data privacy are constantly adapting to keep pace with the rapid innovation in the technologies and business practices of cross-border e-commerce. We intend to issue regular updates to this material as and when merited by changes in legislation in the principal jurisdictions which we cover. More details about how to subscribe for updates are detailed in the last section of this book.

G.E. Kennedy
L.S.P. Prabhu

October 2017

CONTENT OVERVIEW

Chapter One provides an overview of data privacy. Answering a few of the more frequently asked questions, including, who needs a data privacy policy, what is the difference between data privacy and data security and identified areas where liability may arise.

Chapter Two examines data privacy laws in both the U.S. and Canada.

In Chapter Three, the General Data Protection Regulation (GDPR), is introduced. The GDPR, when implemented, will be some of the most stringent data privacy laws worldwide. It would be useful to base your company's privacy policy on the strictest legislation thereby ensuring it fully complies globally.

Chapter Four outlines regional trends around the globe and discusses how data privacy laws differ from country to country, in some cases causing multijurisdictional conflicts.

Chapter Five examines outsourcing, B2B issues and data breach insurance.

In Chapter Six you will find information on what to do in the case of a data privacy breach, how to prevent incidences and reduce risks.

Chapter Seven sets out what substantive provisions should be included in a data privacy policy and how to draft a policy that conforms with the strictest data privacy laws that might be applicable to your business. It includes suggestions on how to streamline your data privacy policy to maximize the compliance in jurisdictions with less rigorous laws.

ABOUT THE AUTHORS

Wendy Kennedy is an international attorney specializing in assisting multinational enterprises in managing their global risks, particularly in relation to compliance, data privacy, and taxation. She is a former university lecturer in international law and is a qualified attorney in the US and UK.

Leighton Peter Prabhu is an accountant and financial advisor who has worked with clients in more than 25 countries. He is particularly experienced in cross-border e-commerce and is a contributing author to the East-West Digital News report "E-Commerce in Russia." He is a regular speaker at international conferences dedicated to digital marketing and e-commerce business development. Peter holds business degrees from McGill University and the University of Cambridge, and completed a certificate in e-commerce at New York University. He is a qualified chartered professional accountant in Canada and holds a CPA certificate from the State of Illinois, USA.

CHAPTER ONE - WHO NEEDS A DATA PRIVACY POLICY?

A. Introduction

Regulation of data protection and data privacy is a murky business, full of conflicting interests and misinformation. This is why many small-to-medium-sized businesses ("SMEs") find it so difficult to decipher what information they should be protecting, much less how to comply with the myriad of regulations. Faced with the knowledge that they should be securing personal data but unsure of how to do so, SMEs often rely on third-party vendors to handle data privacy issues and legal compliance in the hope that such reliance will shield them from liability in the event of a breach of security or unauthorized use of personal information collected. Complete reliance on third-party vendors, however, is misplaced and can be very risky if the SME does not understand its basic responsibilities. Perhaps the most fundamental of these is the obligation to have a strong and legally compliant data privacy policy.

Data privacy policies are necessary in order to be legally compliant but also to assure customers that the company is committed to protecting the privacy of individuals who use the company's website or who buy goods or services from the company. Companies protect such individuals, frequently referred to as the "data subjects," either by agreeing not to share personal information collected with third parties or by giving notice of its plan to do so. Data privacy policies also demonstrate that the company is committed to securing the data it collects in order to prevent theft, loss, or misuse. An SME may conclude that it can avoid the need for a data privacy policy by opting not to collect personal information from data subjects altogether; however, the SME may not realize that something as seemingly harmless as using third-party vendors to process customer payments, for example, can expose them to liability. For that reason, SMEs should also consider appointing a specific person to oversee the development and implementation of. and internal compliance with, a data privacy policy. That person, often referred to as a Data Protection Officer ("DPO") need not devote his or her full-time efforts to the task, but should be able to ensure the company's compliance with the policy and with applicable law.

B. What is the Difference Between Data Privacy and Data Security?

Data Privacy

Data privacy refers to a data subject's *right* or *reasonable expectation* that personally identifiable information will be kept confidential by the party who collects it, unless that party asks for consent, and receives it, or gives notice that it is planning to disclose the information in advance and the data subject does not object. Contemporary notions of data privacy focus on electronic collection, use, and disclosure of personally identifiable information. Different laws governing data privacy have different definitions of "personally identifiable information," but in general, it is a very broad concept and even includes information that, on its own, does not identify a specific person, such as job title with no name attached to it (e.g. banker at First National Bank), but becomes personally identifiable when combined with information from multiple sources (e.g. a first name). Information may come from related or affiliated companies, unrelated companies or even publicly available sources.

Data Security

Data security refers to measures taken to ensure any personally identifiable information is secure from theft or other illegal or unauthorized use. Protective measures can include encryption (making data unreadable to anyone other than intended recipients), authentication (a process for verifying a data subject's identity), a firewall (a system to monitor information flowing into and out of the business through its network), and more. Customers need assurance that a company has processes in place to keep personal data secure in order to feel comfortable when making a purchase from that company, or perhaps accessing services or other online products. Similarly, in a business-to-business setting, other companies are more inclined to do business with a company that understands the importance of safeguarding their information, thereby minimizing the chance of a disruptive data breach.

C. Why Do Businesses Collect Personal Information?

Chances are, businesses with an online presence are collecting information about data subjects regardless of whether they are selling any products or services online. There are many reasons to collect personal information. Of course, when a business makes an online sale it needs to collect the customer's name and address for shipping purposes, if the customer buys a physical product, as well as credit card information for payment. In conjunction with an online purchase, customers frequently have the option to store their payment information with the business for future use. U.S.-based retail giant Amazon, for example, requires its customers to store, at minimum, a default billing address to download and read Kindle eBooks.

Companies also collect information for marketing purposes. As book retailer Barnes & Noble states in its own privacy policy, "We provide personal information to our partners that provide product and service offerings or technologies that we think may be of interest to you."[1] Targeted advertising is one example of how companies put customer information to use. If a data subject searches for a local hardware store, for example, the search itself will generate targeted hardware store advertisements on the data subject's search results page or on another webpage in the near future (e.g. in the case of re-targeting programs). Customer information can also be valuable in developing new products and services—knowing the market's preferences can help increase the chances of successful sales.

Companies don't *just* use customer information for marketing purposes; they also *collect* information on potential customers through various marketing strategies. Such strategies include online sweepstakes and contests, which often involve entry forms asking for detailed personal information. Member loyalty programs can also be part of a successful marketing strategy. Personal information collected through sweepstakes entries, loyalty programs or other "sign-up" marketing techniques target future advertising opportunities while simultaneously building brand identity.

Finally, companies do not just collect information for their own use —they also sell it to third parties for a profit, thereby creating a new revenue stream. The global firm Acxiom is one of the largest data brokerage firms in the world, and its entire business consists of buying and selling data about consumers to help its clients—other companies—target advertising, generate sales, and more.

Of course, Facebook is the most prominent example of a business model based on collecting not only a wide range of personal information but also individual behaviors volunteered by its users, and turning this information to the advantage of its advertisers and marketers.

In a more subtle example of data mining, by default Google's Gmail service scans and analyzes the content of individual messages, and its search engine retains each user's search history. While the company states that the user benefit is a more personalized web browsing experience, the collection of such personal data also adds significant value to Google's legions of advertisers.

Customers, on the other hand, may not want to have their personal information collected, stored, or used outside of the primary transaction through which the data was collected. And the law has recognized the customers' right to control their personal information. In addition, the manner in which the information is stored must be secure, to prevent unwanted access by those who would illegally use private information, such as social security numbers, to open accounts, make charges or otherwise misuse someone else's name or other personal information. Balancing the company's desire to collect customer information with the customer's legitimate interest in maintaining privacy and security over their personal information is one of the main goals of a data privacy policy.

D. Is the Need for a Data Privacy Policy Urgent?

The short answer is, "yes." Data privacy and security are increasingly becoming highly regulated and fines and penalties are stiff. As a recent example, in May 2017, the federal data protection agency, the Commission Nationale de l'Informatique (CNIL), fined Facebook €150,000 for six violations, "including collecting information on users for advertising without having a legal basis". The CNIL also accused the technology group of "'unfair' tracking of people as they browse the Internet, without offering users sufficient warning."[2] Facebook's data collection and handing practices also spurred investigations by Data Protection Authorities (DPAs) in The Netherlands, France, Spain, The City of Hamburg (Germany) and Belgium, prompting calls for the service to amend it practices to come into compliance with EU and country-level data privacy laws.

Consumers have also experienced some success bringing civil claims for damages against companies which retain data privacy policies either not in compliance with the law or where their activities overreach the limitations contained in their own data privacy policies. Moreover, a highly publicized breach of data privacy can undermine consumer confidence, driving customers to competitors with better privacy records.

Two Case Studies: Toysmart and DoubleClick

Consider two of the earliest, and most well-known, cases where consumers sued companies for engaging in business practices that threatened to reveal the consumers' personal information, in breach of existing privacy agreements.

Toysmart

The first of these, which settled in 2000, involved the now-bankrupt online store Toysmart.[3] Through its website, Toysmart.com, the company collected personal customer information on 250,000 individuals that included consumers' names, addresses, billing information, shopping preferences, and family profile information. Its privacy policy stated that personal information collected by the online retailer would never be shared with third parties.

When Toysmart ran into financial difficulties, however, it tried to liquidate its assets, including the customer database, in a sale to the highest bidder. Such sale would have been in breach of the company's own privacy policy. Fearing the example it might set if Toysmart were allowed to auction off its customers' information, the Federal Trade Commission ("FTC") filed a lawsuit against Toysmart claiming unfair or deceptive business practices, invasion of privacy, and violations of the Children's Online Privacy Protection Act of 1998, by collecting names, ages and email addresses of children under the age of 13 without obtaining parental consent.

Though the suit was not brought by a private citizen, the Toysmart litigation was initiated by the FTC in order to protect consumers. The FTC, by virtue of its consumer protection authority, has become one of the U.S. federal government's data privacy watchdogs, and similar actions against companies that fail to respect data privacy or to secure consumer data may find themselves a target. The U.S. Department of Commerce has also filled this role internationally by entering into specific agreements providing for data protection with other nations. An initial example of such measures was the U.S. Safe Harbor Program, which provided a simplified way for U.S. companies to comply with the EU Data Protection Directive and all EU member states' laws implementing the principles set out in the Directive. The EU Data Protection Directive has now been replaced by the General Data Protection Regulation (GDPR) (Regulation (EU) 2016/679) and is explained in Chapter Three. e The U.S. Safe Harbor has been replaced by the EU-U.S. Privacy Shield which imposes tougher obligations on U.S. companies to protect personal information obtained from EU residents and will be discussed more fully in Chapter Two.

DoubleClick

At nearly the same time the Toysmart case was filed in Massachusetts, another case was filed in California by a citizen concerned about action DoubleClick was planning to take regarding its database of customer information.[4] DoubleClick, which maintained a vast data warehouse of information about Internet usage behavior, had acquired a direct-marketing company the prior year and was arranging to link names and addresses from the direct-marketing company with DoubleClick's own information about Internet user behavior. Several class action lawsuits, an FTC probe, and a mass investigation by attorneys general from ten states followed the California lawsuit.

Consumers and regulators were troubled by DoubleClick's plans for a number of reasons. One of the most significant concerns, however, was that DoubleClick's proposal would use "cookies" (digital data that a website stores on a user's browser after the user visits) in a way that severely invaded personal privacy. Although DoubleClick had a data privacy policy in place, it was fairly broad and the FTC eventually found, in its investigation, that DoubleClick did not breach its agreement under the policy. In contrast with Toysmart, then, the issue in the DoubleClick case was not that its actions would be a breach of its privacy policy, but that the business practices allowed under the policy were unreasonable intrusions into data privacy.

In the end, DoubleClick settled the largest of the class action suits against it for $1.8 million. Under the terms of the settlement, DoubleClick also agreed to (1) form a consumer education program focusing on online privacy issues, (2) give clearer notice of its data collection methods, (3) set a five-year expiration date for cookies, (4) obtain express consent before collecting personally identifiable information, and (5) allow outside parties to regularly ensure that DoubleClick was complying with the settlement agreement.

The Lessons

The main message to take away from the cases of Toysmart and DoubleClick are that, not only must your company comply with the terms of its data privacy agreement, but also, those terms should be transparent to consumers and should be reasonable in light of consumers' expectations of privacy of their personal data.

Generally, basic undertakings to be included in a data privacy policy should inform the customer a) that personal information is being collected; b) how personal information will be stored (to ensure security); and c) whether and under what circumstances it will be shared with others. The regulatory trend is to also require that the data subject be notified of changes in the data privacy policy. A sound privacy policy gives rise to customer confidence while ensuring the credibility of the business itself and avoiding costly penalties. What should be included in a data privacy policy is discussed in more detail in Chapter Seven.

The Ability to "Opt-Out"

In light of Toysmart and DoubleClick, companies may wonder whether it is ever legal, or advisable, to sell personal information to third parties. Using an online retailer as an example, let's examine this question. Through its selling process, the online retailer collects significant personal information about its customers. As discussed above under *Why Do Businesses Collect Personal Information?*, the online retailer's ability to resell that information to others, or put the information to its own use, can reap many benefits including the use of targeted advertising of its own products or products sold by affiliated vendors through its website, or the sale of the information to third parties, which creates a new revenue stream for the online retailer.

The online retailer's ability to benefit from the sale of its customers' personal information depends on whether the customers have agreed to allow their personal information to be shared. Popular online retailers take care of consent to information sharing through their privacy policies, which may provide customers with an "opt-out" selection. If customers do not opt-out of agreeing to allow the sharing of their personal information, the online retailer is free to re-use and share its customers' personal information without further notice to the customer.

Contrast this with an "opt-in" selection, which would require customers to affirmatively consent to allowing the online retailer to share their personal data with third parties. Companies generally prefer opt-out notices because people tend not to change the status quo: that is, customers are much less likely to object to the online retailer's sale of personal information if doing so requires them to read the policy, understand how to opt out, and take action to do so.[5] In many countries, opt-out policies do not contravene data policy regulation; in fact, the majority of online retailers use them. As with other data privacy issues, though, the key is transparency. Let your customer know, clearly, what they are opting out of, as well as how they can do so.

By the way, DoubleClick is now owned by the aforementioned Google.

E. Use of Third-Party Vendors

How to Responsibly Choose Third-Party Vendors

If you use a third-party service provider to process personal data for your business, you remain legally responsible for your customers' data privacy and security. In order to ensure you choose third-party service providers which understand this principle and are also committed to data protection, you should:

✓ Consider only service providers with strong reputations for data security and which offer guarantees of their ability to protect your customers' information.

✓ Understand what specific data security measures your service provider has in place and investigate whether it complies with these measures, and has sufficient internal controls.

✓ Ensure your service contract requires the service provider to ask your permission before sub-contracting any aspect of its business that requires handling personal data.

Still think that data privacy isn't a notable issue for your business because you rely on third-party vendors to manage your online business functions? Think again. Many businesses use third-party vendors like Google AdSense or Google Analytics, or one of the many cloud providers and payment portals to supply some website functionality or advertising. Nevertheless, your business is liable for the personal information collected from your customers or website visitors, including liability for breaches by third parties.

Using third-party vendors to track customers comes with its own risks. Consider the following example: you use a third-party service to deliver products or services to a customer. The service provider will need access to information about the customer including, perhaps, information collected by cookies. The information may include the type of browser a customer uses, time spent on the service, language preferences, pages visited and other seemingly anonymous traffic data.

Perhaps your third-party service provider isn't very diligent in following your privacy policy. Perhaps it intentionally ignores it. Either way, it is not hard to imagine a scenario in which your third-party service might also use cookies for unauthorized purposes, like sending advertisements to your customers based on their browsing history or even sharing it with, or selling it to, others without your permission and in violation of your privacy policy. Another possibility is that your third-party service provider may fail to maintain sufficient security measures to protect your customers' personal data, leading to a breach.

Target, one of the largest U.S.-based retailers, experienced one of the largest data breaches in history in late 2013, when it was reported that as many as 110 million credit card, debit cards and personal records were stolen. In early 2014, Target revealed that the likely source of the breach was hackers who stole authentication credentials from a third-party vendor and used them to access Target's systems. Despite the breach arising from a third-party source, it is fairly obvious that Target, and not the vendor, bears the burden of cleaning up after the breach. *Data protection and privacy laws, in almost every case, place responsibility for a third-party breach on the primary business collecting the personal information.*

In order to minimize the risk of liability arising from use of third parties, you should be familiar with the third-party vendor's or service provider's data privacy policies and request changes, if necessary, to maintain compliance with your own policy and with applicable law. Often, large third-party providers (Google Analytics, PayPal, and Amazon, for example) have standardized policies that are not open to negotiation. Nonetheless, you have a duty to be knowledgeable about their policies and to go so far as to switch providers if you are concerned that there is a conflict. Use of third-party vendors or service providers in the cloud computing context is discussed in more detail in Chapter Five.

F. Who's in Charge?

Thus far, we have learned the *what* of data protection: what data security and data privacy are, what a data privacy policy is, and what a policy should contain: information   informing customers of how their personal data will be collected, stored, and used or re-used, disclosing whether personal data will be shared with others, and obtaining consent if necessary. Now, we turn to the *who*: companies need to have a privacy policy, and to maintain compliance with the data protection laws *in each jurisdiction where customers are located*, but *who* will oversee all of these efforts? This is where a Data Protection Officer enters the picture.

What is a Data Protection Officer?

A Data Protection Officer ("DPO") is an individual responsible for advising on the implications of data protection laws, developing a company's data and privacy protection policies and ensuring compliance with the laws. Although the title itself may vary, the appointment of a responsible person is essential. This role could be outsourced or assigned to an in-house employee. If there is no expertise within the business, responsibility for developing a sound privacy policy can be outsourced and, with appropriate training, internal employees can maintain and update the privacy policy as necessary.

**Alternatives to the
Data Protection Officer for SMEs**

You may think your business is too small to warrant the hiring of a full-time DPO. There are some alternatives, however, including:

✓ **A Privacy Committee:** Comprised of employees with a stake in privacy matters. Final responsibility for data privacy should clearly rest with one or a small number of individuals.

✓ **Outside Consultants:** SMEs may benefit enormously, especially when implementing a new data privacy policy, from the guidance of outside firms such as privacy consultants, accounting firms, audit companies, or law firms.

✓ **Industry or Professional Groups:** Several organizations are committed to developing standards, or best practices, in the data security realm. These groups often provide guidance in the form of working papers and seminars.

Who Needs a Data Protection Officer?

With the regulatory climate tightening and legal risks involving personal customer information on the rise, SMEs can no longer afford to ignore privacy issues. It is essential that businesses with an online presence, whether they offer products or services, have a DPO. For smaller companies, the DPO functions may be carried out in conjunction with other job duties. The appointment of a DPO will be mandated by law. An EU Regulation, which represented a substantial overhaul of the current Data Protection Directive set to take effect in 2018, will require appointment of a DPO for all companies with 250 or more employees. The EU Data Protection Directive and General Data Protection Regulation (GDPR)

(Regulation (EU) 2016/679) are discussed in more detail in Chapter Three.

References

[1] Privacy Policy, BARNES & NOBLE BOOKSELLERS (effective Jun. 24, 2017), https://www.barnesandnoble.com/h/help/privacy-policy-complete#q4

[2] Ft.com. (2017). Facebook fined by French regulator over data protection rules. online Available at: https://www.ft.com/content/10f558c6-3a26-11e7-821a-6027b8a20f23?mhq5j=e1 Accessed 24 Jun. 2017.

[3] Fed. Trade Comm'n v. Toysmart.com, LLC, 2000 WL 34016434 (D. Mass. July 21, 2000).

[4] In re Doubleclick, 2001 WL 1029646, No. JC4120 (Cal. Super. Ct. June 11, 2001).

[5] Lynn Chuang Kramer, Private Eyes Are Watching You: Consumer Online Privacy Protection-Lessons from Home and Abroad, 37 TEX. INT'L L.J. 387, 411 (2002)..

CHAPTER TWO - COMPLIANCE WITH DATA PRIVACY LAWS: A SURVEY OF U.S. AND CANADIAN LAW AND MULTIJURISDICTIONAL CONFLICTS

A. Introduction

In this Chapter, we explore the data privacy laws of two other countries that exercise considerable influence in Internet and offline trading: the United States and Canada. While examining U.S. data privacy laws, the EU-U.S. Privacy Shield is also discussed, which provides for freer online trading between these two economies while preserving high standards of data protection for cross-border transfers of personal data. Finally, we review multijurisdictional conflicts in data privacy laws, highlighting the numerous data privacy laws that may be applicable to your business.

B. United States Data Privacy Laws

In the United States there is no single, comprehensive federal law concerning data privacy. Rather, data privacy law in the U.S. consists of a patchwork system of federal and state laws and regulations. data privacy laws are generally aimed at restricting the use of sensitive health and financial information. The following discusses how federal and state laws apply to online data protection and privacy.

Federal Privacy Laws

CAN-SPAM Act of 2003[6]

The CAN-SPAM Act of 2003 applies to all commercial emails, provides email recipients a means to request that they no longer receive emails from a sender, and imposes penalties for violations. CAN-SPAM requires senders of commercial emails to: (1) use transparent header information (i.e. the "to" and "from" fields should be clear and accurate); (2) use clear and accurate subject lines; (3) identify the email as advertising; (4) provide their physical address; (5) give recipients an "opt-out" to stop receiving future emails from the sender; (6) stop sending emails after a customer opts out within 30 days or less; and (7) monitor what third parties are sending you on their behalf, to make sure they are complying as well.

Children's Online Protection Act (1998) ("COPPA")[7]

COPPA was enacted to provide a greater level of protection online for children under 13 years old. The Act seeks to do so by imposing several obligations on commercial website operators and those who provide services online directed to children under 13 and who collect, use, or disclose personal information about those children. The Act also governs website or online service operators who know the information they collect comes from another party directing its services to children under 13. Any such business must:

• Post its privacy policy, which must be clear and comprehensive and must alert users of its information collection practices;

• Give notice directly to parents and get their consent (subject to some exceptions) before collecting a child's personal information online;

• Provide parents the option to allow the child's information to be used internally by the operator but disallowing the provider from disclosing the information to other parties (unless disclosure is essential to the provider's business and the provider makes this clear to parents);

• Give parents the ability to review the child's personal information or to request its deletion;

• Provide parents the ability to stop further online collection or use of the child's personal information;

• Maintain confidentiality, security, and integrity of the information collected; and

• Safely and securely dispose of the information as soon as possible.

The FTC is charged with enforcing COPPA. It investigates and follows up on complaints received by a number of different parties including parents, industry organizations, and consumer groups. COPPA, which was originally enacted in 1998, was amended in December 2012 to modify or expand key definitions within the Rule. The amendments modified the definitions of "operator," "personal information," and "website or online service directed to children." Further, the amendment updated the parental notice and consent requirements, the existing safe harbor provisions, and new safeguard requirements.

The Electronic Communications Privacy Act (1986) ("ECPA")

The ECPA is an umbrella act that includes the Wiretap Act, the Stored Communications Act, and the Pen-Register Act. In passing the ECPA, Congress intended to encourage development of new technologies by assuring potential users of that new technology that their personal data would be protected. The ECPA was additionally intended to provide "a fair balance between the privacy expectations of citizens and the legitimate needs of law enforcement."[8]

Both the Wiretap Act and the Pen-Register Act govern surveillance of Internet communications that are "in transit," while the Stored Communications Act governs retrieval of stored communications. All three Acts under the ECPA make it a federal crime to "capture the communications of others" through wiretap or other means without first obtaining consent of the parties or a court's approval. A number of exemptions apply to this general rule, including one exemption that gives the U.S. government the power to directly access information or to require a third party to turn it over.

Penalties for violating the ECPA include a maximum of five years' jail time and a $250,000 fine. Injured parties may recover from the violator actual damages, punitive damages (damages meant to "punish" the defendant), and attorney's fees. The U.S. government cannot be sued for violation of the ECPA; however, evidence the government gathers illegally under the ECPA cannot be used in court.

Critics have not been shy in voicing strong opposition to the ECPA in the years since its passage. Most notably, the exponential growth in technology since 1986, when the Act was passed, and the present day has left the Act as an increasingly inadequate response to the needs of both law enforcement and the private sector. Courts have treated information stored on home computers differently than information stored in the cloud, for example, making significant reform of ECPA all the more urgent.

Congress is considering the "Email Privacy Act" (H.R. 387) which passed the House of Representatives in early 2017 and is now before the Senate Judiciary Committee. The Act proposes to amend the ECPA to extend the warrant requirement to communications stored for more than 180 days. An earlier version of the Act would have required notice of email searches to the user, with some exceptions.[9]

Fair and Accurate Credit Transactions Act (2003) ("FACTA")[10]

FACTA, enacted in December 2003, was U.S. Congress' response to industry groups and consumer advocates who expressed concern with the prior legislation regulating credit transactions, the Fair Credit Reporting Act (the "FCRA"). Like the FCRA, FACTA requires consumer credit reports, and access to such reports, to comply with standards that are consistent nationwide. FACTA also provides new means to protect consumers' personal information, aimed at fighting identity theft, preserving privacy, providing freer access to individuals' information retained by credit bureaus, and improving the accuracy of consumer reports.

Many U.S. consumers may be aware that, under FACTA, they are entitled to receive one free credit report per year from each of the three major credit reporting agencies. Additionally, under FACTA, mortgage lenders are required to divulge to consumers different factors, including credit scores, which influence a consumer's mortgage loan terms.

How to Join the EU-U.S. Privacy Shield Program

If you are a U.S.-based business interested in joining the EU-U.S. Privacy Shield program, the U.S. Department of Commerce recommends that you take the following steps before sending your self-certification form to the Department:

- ✓ Confirm that your business is subject to the jurisdiction of the U.S. FTC or Department of Transportation ("DoT")

- ✓ Develop a privacy policy that complies with the EU-U.S. Privacy Shield Program requirements. Including stating that the privacy policy adheres to the Privacy Shield Principles.

- ✓ Provide a hyperlink to an independent recourse mechanism able to investigate unresolved complaints.

- ✓ Provide accurate location of your Privacy Policy.

- ✓ Assign one person in your company to be in charge of addressing Safe Harbor issues including questions, complaints, and requests for access.

For more information on each step, visit
https://www.commerce.gov/page/eu-us-privacy-shield
http://export.gov/safeharbor/eu/eg_main_018495.asp

The EU-U.S. and Swiss-U.S. Privacy Shield Frameworks

The EU-US Privacy Shield represents a replacement for the U.S-E.U. Safe Harbor Agreement which the European Court of Justice in its ruling on 6 October 2015, declared invalid.[11] The new arrangement places stronger obligations on U.S. companies to protect the personal data of Europeans and stronger monitoring and enforcement obligations by the U.S. Department of Commerce and Federal Trade Commission (FTC). The U.S.-EU and U.S.-Swiss Safe Harbor Frameworks are no longer legally recognized as adequate under EU and Swiss law therefore an entity transferring personal data from the European Union and Switzerland to the United States will be in violation of relevant E.U. and Swiss law.

The Privacy Shield program, enables U.S.-based organizations to join one or both of the Privacy Shield Frameworks (The EU-U.S. or Swiss-U.S. Privacy Shield Frameworks). An organization who wishes to benefit from Privacy Shield certification will be required to self-certify to the Department of Commerce and publicly commit to comply with the Framework's requirements. Although joining Privacy Shield is voluntary, once an eligible organization makes the public commitment to comply with the Framework's requirements, the commitment will become enforceable under U.S. law.

The Requirements can be found here:

https://www.privacyshield.gov/article?id=Requirements-of-Participation

State Privacy Laws

There is little uniformity as to data protection and privacy legislation from state to state throughout the U.S. Additionally, federal laws— FACTA, for example—preempt state law. This means that, where a federal and state law conflict, the federal law will "trump" the state law. As one might expect, and similarly to what has occurred in the EU, this web of state laws, each separately addressing privacy concerns, results in fragmentation. Notwithstanding the compliance difficulties companies face as a result of this fragmentation, states continue to pass their own data privacy laws and to amend them in light of constantly developing technology. Legislation of one of the states that has been called a "pioneer on digital privacy laws"[12]— California—is explored below.

California State Online Privacy Laws

California Online Privacy Protection Act ("CalOPPA"), effective July 1, 2004, was one of the first to require companies collecting personal information online from California residents to post their privacy policies conspicuously and to comply with the terms of their policies. Under CalOPPA, a privacy policy must: (1) identify categories of personal data collected; (2) identify categories of third parties with whom the personal data may be shared; (3) describe the process for reviewing and requesting changes to one's own personal data (if available) and notify customers if there is no process; (4) describe the process for notification of changes to the privacy policy; and (5) identify its effective date.

Senate Bill 1386 ("SB 1386") Security Breach Information Act, effective July 1, 2003, requires any business that stores unencrypted personal data of a California resident to notify each customer in the event of a security breach. SB 1386 identifies personal information as a person's first name or initial and last name. This information, in unencrypted form, includes combined data such as a Californian resident's driver's license number, social security number or any other identifying personal information, that is any information which alone does not identify a specific individual, but when combined with other information can lead to identification of a specific individual. Unlike the EU Data Protection Directive, however, personal information does not include any information that is lawfully made available to the public such as government, local, state, or federal records.

SB 1386 was the first state law requiring data breach notification. Since its adoption, nearly every other state has followed suit and passed its own breach notification law.

Senate Bill 46 ("SB 46"), an amendment to SB 1386, SB 46 expands website operators' breach notification requirements to include instances of theft, loss, or unintentional disclosure of an Internet user's login name and password of email accounts as well as social networking sites and online games. SB 46 took effect on January 1, 2014. Although as a state law, SB 46 only requires notification of breaches to California residents, many website operators may find it difficult or cumbersome to distinguish between California and non-California residents. Therefore, the law may have the effect of increasing situations in which data breaches are reported to all users, regardless of where they live.

Assembly Bill 370 ("AB 370"), the Do Not Track Amendment to CalOPPA, passed in September 2013, requires website operators and online service providers to disclose on their sites how they handle "do not track" signals. "Do not track" signals are web browsing preference settings that users can choose to tell websites that they do not want to be tracked. If website operators can correctly interpret and abide by these settings, personal information will not be collected about the individual who chooses affirmatively not to be tracked. AB 370, however, does not require website operators and service providers to obey these settings; instead, the bill obligates the website to disclose how it treats these signals.

Assembly Bill 1291 ("AB 1291"), the Right to Know Act of 2013, as proposed, gives consumers a right to see all information a website operator or online service provider has collected about them. Although a standard right under the EU Data Directives, consumers' ability to receive information collected about themselves online is virtually nonexistent in the U.S. AB 1291 expands the scope of consumer access significantly—and may create compliance problems for businesses—in three ways: (1) it expands the definition of personal data to include IP addresses, device identifiers for smart phones, and other things; (2) it requires disclosure of all personal data, including those easily and not-so-easily accessible from the business' point of view; and (3) it provides statutory fines and permits private parties to sue for violations.

U.S. State Data Breach Notification Law

Currently, 48 states, as well as the District of Columbia, Puerto Rico and the US Virgin Islands all have enacted laws requiring notification of security breaches involving personal information. A majority of these laws focus on handling a data breach after it has occurred, whereas a growing portion of data breach laws have taken steps to mandate preventive measures.

U.S. Anti-Spam Legislation

Most U.S. states have enacted specific anti-spam laws. States that have not passed specific laws often address the same concerns through unlawful business and trade practices laws, anti-solicitation laws, or laws relating to cyber crimes. The primary goal of the laws is to place limitations on unsolicited commercial email and develop a process to allow consumers to instruct the sender to stop any further emails. The state's attorney general is generally responsible for enforcing a state-specific anti-spam law, although many laws provide individual parties with the right to sue for violations as well. It is worth reiterating that the federal CAN-SPAM Act of 2003 (discussed earlier in this Chapter) preempts, or takes precedence over, state anti-spam laws.

C. Canadian Data Privacy Laws

In Canada, data privacy laws are generally aimed at balancing an individual's right to privacy of their personal information with an organization's need to gather, use, and occasionally disclose that information. Canadian federal data privacy Three primary federal statutes govern use and disclosure of personal information in Canada: the *Personal Information Protection Electronic Documents Act* ("PIPEDA")[13] (establishes the rules regarding how private-sector organizations. must handle personal information in the course of commercial activity), the **Privacy Act**[14] (covers the personal information-handling practices of federal government departments and agencies), and the **Access to Information Act**[15] (provides a right of access to information in records under the control of a government institution). Oversight of federal data protection laws lies with the Privacy Commissioner of Canada, who collects and investigates complaints.

In addition to the three chief federal Acts governing use of personal information, each Canadian province and territory has enacted data privacy laws giving individuals the right to access and correct personal information collected about them by their local governments. Provincial and territorial governments have also enacted data privacy legislation dealing with specific industries, like health care and banking. Oversight of provincial and territorial information laws rests with an independent commissioner or ombudsman.[16]

Private Sector Data Privacy Regulations

Canadian businesses are subject to federal or provincial privacy protection legislation governing both customer and (with some exceptions) employee information. The foundational regulation Canadian privacy laws are built on is the Canadian Standards Association Model Privacy Code (1996).[17]

Canadian Standards Association Model Privacy Code (1996)

Canada's first data privacy regulation of private sector businesses came in the form of a model code developed by the Canadian Standards Association (the "CSA"; a nonprofit that develops standards in over fifty areas) in conjunction with government, consumers, and industry participants. The Canadian Standards Association Model Privacy Code (1996), which was not legally binding on organizations, was nonetheless notable for its status as the first voluntary national standard for data privacy developed by any country.

Personal Information Protection Electronic Documents Act (2000) ("PIPEDA")

Less than five years after the completion of the CSA Model Privacy Code, Canada's federal government passed Bill C-6, also known as the Personal Information Protection Electronic Documents Act. Although new in name, PIPEDA represented the continuation of prior regulation in two ways. First, it incorporated the ten foundational principles of the CSA Model Privacy Code into Schedule 1 of the Act, which are the Act's substantive privacy provisions. The ten principles are:

- Accountability: by organizations for information under their control;

- Identifying Purposes: during or before information collection;

- Consent: of the individual giving the information;

- Limiting Collection: to what is necessary and lawful for the purpose;

- Limiting Use, Disclosure, and Retention: to the purpose for which it was collected;

• Accuracy: of information is important;

• Safeguards: should be in place to protect information from misuse;

• Openness: of an organization's privacy policies and practices;

• Individual Access: of records for review and correction by individual owners of the information; and

• Challenging Compliance: the organization should provide the means to challenge an organization's compliance with these principles.

The second way in which PIPEDA represents the carryover of prior legislation is its patterning after the EU Data Protection Directive. The EU Data Protection Directive outlines privacy principles for the processing of data which include:

1) Notice– (Article 10) The data subject must be provided with the identity of the data controller, the purposes for which data is collected and third party recipients

2) Choice– (Article 14) The data subject may object to the processing of their personal data for the purpose of direct marketing and the disclosure of data for third parties or uses.

3) Access and Correction– (Article 12) The data subject may request to view data an entity has on record about them and rectify, erase of block the processing of data if incorrect or incomplete.

4) Data Quality– (Article 6) Data should be processed lawfully. It should be collected and processed for specific and legitimate purposes. Data should be timely, accurate and complete. Data that is no longer necessary should be kept in a format that is not personally identifiable.

5) Data Security– (Article 17) Appropriate steps must be taken to protect against accidental loss, and unauthorized access, use or destruction.[18]

Canada, like numerous other countries, recognized that EU member nations represent significant markets for its country's goods and services. Bringing its own data privacy laws into compliance with the EU Directive was desirable, therefore, to ensure that Canadian organizations could exchange information with EU-based entities (by providing data warehousing services for EU businesses, for example).

As discussed earlier, the EU Directive instructs member nations to allow data transfers of personal information to countries outside the EU only when "adequate protection" for the information exists. Thus, non-EU nations that fail to maintain data protection laws that conform to the EU Directive's mandates will find the transfer of personal information between countries blocked. Fortunately for Canada, its attempt to model PIPEDA after the EU to bring itself into compliance with the EU Directive proved successful. In December 2001, the European Commission announced that PIPEDA provided personal information an "adequate level of protection."[19] With this ruling, Canada became the first non-EU nation to meet the data transfer standard of the EU Directive.

The following are some of the main features of PIPEDA:

Rationale: According to Part 1, section 3 of the Act, PIPEDA seeks to establish, "in an era in which technology increasingly facilitates the circulation and exchange of information," laws that recognize an individual's right to privacy of their personal information as well as an organization's legitimate need to "collect, use or disclose" personal information in certain circumstances, so long as they are subject to restrictions governing the personal information's collection, use, or disclosure. Unlike EU data privacy law, which is very favorable toward individual rights, PIPEDA represents a more business-friendly approach. One United Nations official has said that PIPEDA's stated purpose represents "a remarkable effort not to place an enormous burden on the private entrepreneurial sector."[20]

PIPEDA's Application

PIPEDA covers the following entities with regard to their collection, use or disclosure of personal information:

1. organizations that are deemed to be a 'federal work, consumer and employee personal information practices of undertaking or business' (e.g. banks, telecommunications companies, airlines, railways, and other interprovincial undertakings)

2. organizations who collect, use and disclose personal information in the course of a commercial activity.

Covered Organizations: PIPEDA applies to "organizations," which is broadly defined in Part 1 section (2) of the Act to mean "an association, a partnership, a person and a trade union."[21] PIPEDA does not apply to (a) government entities covered by the Canadian Privacy Act (discussed further below).

Covered Transactions: PIPEDA applies to "organizations,"[22] who collect, use, or disclose "personal information"[23] in the course of "commercial activities."[24] The Act expressly excludes the following organizations engaged in the following transactions from coverage:

(a) any government institution to which the Privacy Act applies;

(b) any individual in respect of personal information that the individual collects, uses or discloses for personal or domestic purposes and does not collect, use or disclose for any other purpose; or

(c) any organization in respect of personal information that the organization collects, uses or discloses for journalistic, artistic or literary purposes and does not collect, use or disclose for any other purpose.[25]

The primary question to be answered regarding whether an organization is subject to the Act depends on whether the organization's data collection *activity* falls under the category of "commercial activity." The Act defines commercial activity as "any particular transaction, act or conduct or any regular course of conduct that is of a commercial character, including the selling, bartering or leasing of donor, membership or other fundraising lists."[26] In this context, "commercial" is broadly construed and includes selling or leasing membership, donor, or fundraising lists, which may be critical components of nonprofit fundraising activity.

Definition of Personal Information: Like the EU Directive, PIPEDA defines "personal information" in an extremely broad fashion. Under PIPEDA, personal information is defined as "information about an identifiable individual." Information that falls under this definition identifies an individual. The individual need not be directly identified by the information; it is enough if the individual can be identified by matching the information with information available from other sources. The most common application of PIPEDA involves personal data such as first name or initials, last name, e-mail address, phone numbers, credit reports, and education records. "Personal information" has been found to include medical or biological data,[28] biometric data,[29] the sound of one's voice,[30] or photographic or video images.[31]

Retroactive Nature of PIPEDA: PIPEDA is *retroactive*, meaning its terms apply to information obtained before the enactment of the Act. Thus, an organization interested in using or disclosing earlier-collected information must still obtain the proper consent from the individual. Additionally, the Act applies to non-Canadian organizations seeking to collect, use or disclose information about Canadians. "A U.S. company looking to use a Canadian's personal data," then, "will have to obtain consent from the individual, even if the data were collected years ago."[32]

The Digital Privacy Act: On the Canadian government approved amendments to PIPEDA through Bill S-4 or the Digital Privacy Act.[33] The Digital Privacy Act will be enacted in two phases. The first phase involved amendments to PIPEDA with immediate effect, whereas those provisions relating to data breaches will come into force following associated regulations being developed.

One of the most significant aspects of the amendments which had immediate effect involved a new requirement for valid consent. The amended consent provisions found in section 6.1 provides "is only valid if it is reasonable to expect that an individual to whom the organization's activities are directed would understand the nature, purpose and consequences of the collection, use or disclosure of the personal information to which they are consenting"[34] The import of this new consent requirement is that organizations should tailor consent "to whom the organization's activities are directed", restated this is an objective standard in that the terms of consent should be understandable by their target audience particularly children or other vulnerable populations.

The amendments to PIPEDA that come into force once other supporting regulations are put in place speak to organizations' obligations regarding data breaches. The main provisions regarding data breaches include more rigorous obligations regarding keeping records of breaches and security safeguards; notifying affected individuals about data breaches and an obligation on the part of organizations to notify third parties if the third party could mitigate the risk of harm to the affected individual arising from a data breach.

Exemption of Provinces with "Substantially Similar" Laws: Under PIPEDA, the federal government has the power to declare that certain organizations, activities, or classes are exempt from Part 1 of the Act (regulating personal information collected, used, or disclosed in commercial activity and personal information about employees) if the Canadian province in which the organization is located has "substantially similar" data privacy laws.

As of the date of publication, the following data privacy acts Columbia were accorded "substantial similarity" status.

Personal Information Protection Act (British Columbia)[35]

Personal Information Protection Act (Alberta)[36]

An Act Respecting the Protection of Personal Information in the Private Sector (Québec)[37]

Personal Health Information Protection Act (Ontario)[38]

Personal Health Information Privacy and Access Act (New Brunswick)[39]

Personal Health Information Act (Nova Scotia)[40]

Personal Health Information Act (Newfoundland and Labrador)[41]

Public Sector

The Canadian Privacy Act (1983)

Unlike PIPEDA, the Canadian Privacy Act regulates the collection of personal information by the government. The Act was passed in 1983 to "protect the privacy of individuals with respect to personal information about themselves held by a government institution."[42] The Privacy Act replaced and amended parts of the Canadian Human Rights Act. Under the Privacy Act, individuals are given the right to access and inspect information collected about them by the federal government.

Personal information under the Act is defined even more expansively than under PIPEDA as "information about an identifiable individual that is recorded in any form."[43] The Supreme Court of Canada pointed out in a 1997 case that the definition was intentionally broad, and "entirely consistent with the great pains that have been taken to safeguard individual liberty."[44]

The Privacy Act requires a government institution to only collect personal information when it directly relates to the entity's activities or one of its operating programs. The government should collect the information directly from the individual when possible. Additionally, the individual should be informed about the purpose of the information collection. "In the interests of transparency and openness," government entities must publish data disclosing the different information banks they maintain.[45] The Act does allow limited use and disclosure of personal information without the consent of the individual for purposes of national security, law enforcement, and the like.

Proposed Reforms: The Privacy Act has not undergone substantive revision since its enactment in 1983.

In March 2016, the <u>Standing Committee on Access to Information, Privacy and Ethics</u> announced it was undertaking a <u>study</u> of the Privacy Act Canada's federal public sector privacy law, which has remained largely unchanged since it was proclaimed in 1983.

The Office of the Privacy Commissioner of Canada (OPC) offered its recommendations and are as follows:

Theme One: Technological Changes

1. Clarify requirements for information-sharing agreements: Require that all information sharing under paragraphs 8(2)(a) and (f) of the Privacy Act be governed by written agreements and that these agreements include specified elements. Further, all new or

amended agreements should be submitted to the Office of the Privacy Commissioner of Canada (OPC) for review, and existing agreements should be reviewable upon request. Finally, departments should be required to be transparent about the existence of these agreements.

2. Create a legal obligation for government institutions to safeguard personal information: Create an explicit requirement for institutions to safeguard personal information with appropriate physical, organizational and technological measures commensurate with the level of sensitivity of the data.

3. Make breach reporting mandatory: Create an explicit requirement for government institutions to report material breaches of personal information to the OPC in a timely manner and to notify affected individuals in appropriate cases.

Theme Two: Legislative Modernization

4. Create an explicit necessity requirement for collection: Amend section 4 of the Privacy Act to create a more explicit necessity requirement for the collection of personal information, consistent with other privacy laws in Canada and abroad;

5. Replace the ombudsman model for the investigation of complaints with OPC powers to issue binding orders;

6. Consider creating a statutory mechanism to independently review privacy complaints against the OPC;

7. Require government institutions to conduct privacy impact assessments (PIAs) for new or significantly amended programs and submit them to OPC prior to implementation;

8. Require government institutions to consult with OPC on draft legislation and regulations with privacy implications before they are tabled;

9. Provide OPC with an explicit public education and research mandate: Add a provision to the Privacy Act explicitly conferring the Privacy Commissioner with a mandate to undertake public education and research activities in respect of public sector privacy issues;

10. Require an ongoing five year review of the Act.

Theme 3: Enhancing Transparency

11. Grant the Privacy Commissioner discretion to publicly report on government privacy issues when in the public interest: Amend section 64 of the Act to create an exemption from confidentiality requirements to allow the Privacy Commissioner to report publicly on government privacy issues where he considers it in the public interest to do so.

12. Expand the Commissioner's ability to share information with counterparts domestically and internationally to facilitate enforcement collaboration.

13. Provide the Privacy Commissioner with discretion to discontinue or decline complaints in specified circumstances: Amend section 32 of the Act to grant the Commissioner with discretion to decline complaints or discontinue investigations on specified grounds, including when the complaint is frivolous, vexatious or made in bad faith.

14. Strengthen transparency reporting requirements for government institutions: Strengthen reporting requirements on broader privacy issues dealt with by federal organizations as well as specific transparency requirements for lawful access requests made by agencies involved in law enforcement.

15. Extend coverage of the Act: Amend the Act to extend coverage to all government institutions, including Ministers'

Offices and the Prime Minister's Office, and extend rights of access to foreign nationals.

16. Limit exemptions to access to personal information requests under the Act: Exemptions to personal information access requests should be limited. They should generally be injury-based and discretionary to maximize disclosure.[46]

The Access to Information Act (1983) ("AIA")

Canada's Access to Information Act is complementary to its Privacy Act, and was also passed in 1983. Unlike the Privacy Act, which governs access to personal information by the individual, the AIA governs access to information in general. Like the Privacy Act, the general goal of the AIA is "to make government more open and transparent, allowing citizens to more fully participate in the democratic process."[47] Under the AIA, individuals and corporations have the right to request access to records controlled by the federal government.

Requests for access to information are to be made in writing to the governmental body that has control of the record. The request should also include enough detail to help an experienced employee find the record with reasonable effort. If the government entity refuses to grant access to the information, it must provide in writing the reason for its refusal and inform the person who made the request of their right to submit a complaint regarding the refusal to the Information Commissioner, the governmental position created to help individuals challenge federal entities' actions under the AIA.

Proposed Reforms: In the 30 years since the passage of the AIA, there have been numerous minor reforms to, and criticisms of, the Act. A 2008 report and another report in 2010 compared Canada's Access to Information Act to other freedom of information laws around the globe. Both found Canada to be significantly trailing other nations in providing access to government information. Despite these indicators of flaws in the Act, it has not undergone a substantial overhaul since it was first enacted. In October 2013, Canada's national information and privacy commissioners and the provincial commissioners released a joint resolution offering suggestions for modernizing the country's access to information and privacy laws. Days later, Canadian Federal Information Commissioner Suzanne Legault advised that without significant reforms to the AIA, "the health of our Canadian democracy is at risk."[48] As of the date of publication no reforms have been enacted since the 2013 joint resolution.

References

[6] Pub. L. No. 108–187, 117 Stat. 2699 (2003) (codified at 15 U.S.C. §§ 7701-13). Available at https://www.gpo.gov/fdsys/pkg/PLAW-108publ187/html/PLAW-108publ187.htm

[7] Pub. L. No. 105-277, 112 Stat. 2681-728 (1998) (Codified at 15 U.S.C. §§ 6501-05).

[8] *Electronic Communications Privacy Act*, ELEC. PRIVACY INFO. CTR., http://epic.org/privacy/ecpa/#background (last visited June 24, 2017).

[9] https://www.congress.gov/bill/115th-congress/house-bill/387

[10] Codified in scattered sections of 15 U.S.C. and 20 U.S.C.

[11] (Case C-362/14 – Maximillian Schrems v Irish Data Protection Commissioner).

[12] Somini Sengupta, *No U.S. Action, So States Move on Privacy Law*, N.Y. TIMES, Oct. 31, 2013, at A1, *available at* http://www.nytimes.com/2013/10/31/technology/no-us-action-so-states-move-on-privacy-law.html?_r=0

[13] Personal Information Protection and Electronic Documents Act (S.C. 2000, c. 5) available at http://laws-lois.justice.gc.ca/eng/acts/P-8.6/index.html

[14] Privacy Act (R.S.C., 1985, c. P-21) available at http://laws-lois.justice.gc.ca/eng/acts/P-21/FullText.html . PIPEDA was amended in 2015 by the Digital Privacy Act Digital Privacy Act (S.C. 2015, c. 32) (formerly known as Bill S-4) available at http://laws-lois.justice.gc.ca/eng/annualstatutes/2015_32/FullText.html The Digital Privacy

Act, received Royal Assent in June 2015, resulting in a number of significant amendments to PIPEDA. Many of the Amendments came into force in June 2015 while those relating to "breaches of security safeguards" (which generally include incidents commonly referred to as data breaches) will come into force following associated regulations being developed and put into place by the federal government.

[15] Access to Information Act (R.S.C., 1985, c. A-1) available at http://laws-lois.justice.gc.ca/eng/acts/a-1/

[16] The Office of the Privacy Commissioner provides a list of each commissioner or ombudsperson responsible for overseeing provincial and territorial privacy legislation. The list is available at https://www.priv.gc.ca/en/about-the-opc/what-we-do/provincial-and-territorial-collaboration/provincial-and-territorial-privacy-laws-and-oversight/

[17] Model Code for the Protection of Personal Information (CAN/CSA-Q830-96; published March 1996; reaffirmed 2001) available at http://cmcweb.ca/eic/site/cmc-cmc.nsf/eng/fe00076.html

[18] European Union, Directive 95/46/EC of the European Parliament and of the Council on the Protection of Individuals with Regard to the Processing of Personal Data and on the Free Movement of Such Data, 24 October 1995, available at: http://www.refworld.org/docid/3ddcc1c74.html accessed 22 June 2017

[19] *Frequently Asked Questions on the Commission's adequacy finding on the Canadian Personal Information Protection and Electronic Documents Act*, EUROPEAN COMM'N, http://ec.europa.eu/justice/policies/privacy/thridcountries/adequacy-faq_en.htm (last visited Jan. 17, 2014).

[20] Ruwantissa Abeyratne, *Attacks on America-Privacy Implications of Heightened Security Measures in the United States, Europe, and Canada*, 67 J. AIR L. & COM. 83, 109 (2002).

[21] Personal Information Protection and Electronic Documents Act, S.C. 2000, s. (2) (1) (Can.) hereinafter PIPEDA, *available at* http://laws-lois.justice.gc.ca/eng/acts/P-8.6/index.html .

[22] *Id.* at s. Note that this does not necessarily mean that nonprofit (*i.e.* "non-commercial") *organizations* do not have to comply with PIPEDA's terms. *Id. at pt 1*

[23] *Id. at* s. (2)

[24] Note that this does not necessarily mean that nonprofit (*i.e.* "non-commercial") *organizations* do not have to comply with PIPEDA's terms.

[25] *Id.* at (4)(2)(a)-(c)

[26] *Id.* at s. (2)

[27] *Id.* at pt. 1 c. 2.

[28] Rousseau v. Wyndowe, 2006 FC 1312 (F.C.)

[29] Yeager v. Canada (Minister of Citizenship and Immigration), 2008 FC 113 (F.C.).

[30] Wansink v. Telus Communications Inc, 2007 FCA 21.

[31] Eastmond v. Canadian Pacific Railway, 2004 FC 852. For an extensive discussion of the scope of personal information under the Act see Scassa, T. (2015). Privacy and publicly available personal information. Canadian Journal of Law and Technology, 11(1).

[32] LEGAL ASPECTS OF INTERNATIONAL SOURCING § 1:66.

[33] Digital Privacy Act, SC 2015, c 32, available at http://canlii.ca/t/52m26.

[34] *Id. at s. (6.1)*

[35] PERSONAL INFORMATION PROTECTION ACT SBC 2003 CHAPTER 63 available   at http://www.bclaws.ca/Recon/document/ID/freeside/00_03063_01#part1

[36] Freedom of Information and Protection of Privacy Act, RSA 2000 available at http://www.qp.alberta.ca/1266.cfm?page=2003_366.cfm&leg_type=Regs&isbncln=9780779749003

[37] An Act respecting the Protection of Personal Information in the Private Sector, CQLR c P-39.1, available at http://canlii.ca/t/l031

[38] Personal Health Information Protection Act, 2004, S.O. 2004, c. 3, Sched. A available at https://www.ontario.ca/laws/statute/04p03

[39] Personal Health Information Privacy and Access Act, SNB 2009, c P-7.05, available at http://canlii.ca/t/52xx0

[40] Personal Health Information Act, SNS 2010, c 41, available at http://canlii.ca/t/52pkj

[41] Personal Health Information Act, SNL 2008, c P-7.01, http://canlii.ca/t/52wvx

[42] Elana Rivkin-Haas, *Electronic Medical Records and the Challenge to Privacy: How the United States and Canada Are Responding*, 34 HASTINGS INT'L & COMP. L. REV. 177, 194 (2011).

[43] *Id.*

[44] *Id.*

[45] *Id.*

[46] Priv.gc.ca. (2017). Review of the Privacy Act - Revised recommendations - Office of the Privacy Commissioner of Canada. online Available at:

https://www.priv.gc.ca/en/privacy-topics/privacy-laws-in-canada/the-privacy-act/pa_r/pa_ref_rec_161101/ Accessed 26 Jun. 2017. *Id.*

[47] *Access to information and privacy at CIC* Citizenship and Immigrant Canada, GOV'T OF CAN., http://www.cic.gc.ca/english/DEPARTMENT/atip/index.asp (last visited Jan. 18, 2014); *see also Access to Information*, TREASURY BD. OF CAN. SECRETARIAT, http://www.tbs-sct.gc.ca/atip-aiprp/tools/administration-application-eng.asp (last visited Jan. 18, 2014).

[48] Andrea Janus, *Problems with Access-To-Information System Put 'Canadian Democracy At Risk': Legault*, CTV NEWS (Oct. 17, 2013, 11:10 AM), http://www.ctvnews.ca/canada/problems-with-access-to-information-system-put-canadian-democracy-at-risk-legault-1.1501069

CHAPTER THREE - EU DATA PROTECTION LEGISLATION

A. Introduction

By now, we have established the importance of having a data privacy policy and the need to be in strict legal compliance when it comes to protecting any personal information. Because the legal requirements businesses face often shape the information included in a data privacy policy, it is helpful to examine some of the data protection laws currently in place before turning to specific elements to be included in a data privacy policy. Data protection legislation in the European Union ("EU") provides a particularly good model to study, both because it sets the bar for protecting personal information higher than almost anywhere else in the world and because many other jurisdictions—Hong Kong, Canada, and parts of Latin America, for example—have modeled their own data protection laws after the EU's.

Beginning with the Data Protection Directive of 1995, the EU enacted a series of Directives (legislation "directed" at guiding implementation of EU principles into the laws of Member States) dealing with the regulation of data protection and privacy, both offline and online. Because each Member State was free to enact its own laws under the Directives, so long as those laws followed the general principles in the Directives, inconsistencies inevitably developed among the various Member States. As a result, organizations that collect and process data in multiple Member States have faced conflicts and administrative burdens. Consequently, the European Commission, which is the EU's primary administrative institution, drafting proposals for new laws, implementing policies, proposed a new Data Protection Regulation in 2012, which, if passed, will impose more specific and uniform rules regarding data protection on the Member States. It would require implementation of the Regulation as drafted rather than re-interpreted into local law.

EU Historical Concern for Data Privacy and Protection

European nations have long been concerned with protection of personal information. After the Second World War, a time during which databases of personal information were used to segregate populations and commit atrocities against targeted groups, European nations entered into several international agreements recognizing the right to privacy of personal information as a fundamental human right. Today, the number of laws addressing protection and privacy of personal information and the breadth of the material these laws cover shows that the EU continues to be deeply committed to protecting personal information. In addition to the Directives mentioned above, the following legislation illustrates the importance of data protection in the EU:

• Convention 108 of The Council of Europe, The Convention for the Protection of Individuals with regard to Automatic Processing of Personal Data[49];

• Article 16 of the Treaty on the Functioning of the European Union[50];

• European Convention for the Protection of Human Rights and Fundamental Freedoms[51];

• The Charter of Fundamental Rights of the European Union[52]; and

• Commission Regulation 45/2001,[53] regulating the processing of personal information by governmental bodies.

B. The Directives

As noted above, EU Directives generally set out agreed principles and leave the Member States to "transpose" the principles in the Directives into laws within their own countries. Thus, while the laws transposed by the EU Member States do incorporate the underlying principles, there is fragmentation, which has led to confusion and uncertainty for businesses. Nonetheless, the Directives have been fundamental in shaping data protection laws in the EU and across the globe.

The Data Protection Directive (Directive 95/46/EC), enacted in October 1995, regulates the processing of data within the EU. The principles set out in this Directive are aimed at the protection of fundamental rights and freedoms in the processing of personal data. The principles establish the need for the accuracy of data collected; provide for notification and legitimacy of its collection and use; create guidelines for the processing of special categories of sensitive information; require identification of the "data controller" (the person at a company, or the company itself, who decides for what purpose personal data is to be collected and in what manner), and call for identification of recipients; impose a right of access to the data by the data subject; identify restrictions or exemptions such as national security; provide a process to object; provide for confidentiality and security of processing; create a national supervisory authority; provide for a judicial remedy; and permit transfer of personal data to a third country only if such country maintains an equivalent standard of protection. A more complete explanation of these principles follows later in this Chapter.

Directive on Privacy and Electronic Communications (Directive 2002/58/EC) is intended to complement the Data Protection Directive by applying its principles to electronic communications. This Directive requires electronic communications providers to ensure the security of personal information and the confidentiality of communications, sets guidelines for retention and destruction of personal information, and requires express consent, through an opt-in selection, before unsolicited commercial communications can be made. Unsolicited commercial communications include text messages, email, and automated calling systems. The Directive provides for the imposition of penalties and other legal sanctions for breach of its provisions.

Data Retention Directive (Directive 2006/24/EC, amending Article 15 of Directive 2002/58/EC), effective May 2006, was intended to make obligations imposed on providers of publicly available electronic communications services and networks more uniform among the EU Member States. Specifically, the Directive sought to ensure the providers of these services retained certain data so they would be available for investigation, detection, and prosecution of serious crimes.

Citizens' Rights Directive or the "Cookie Directive" (Directive 2009/136/EC, amending Directive 2002/58/EC), enacted in 2009, sets out guidelines for the use of analytic tools, such as cookies, and includes new obligations on electronic communications service providers to report security breaches to the competent national authority.

Taken together, these Directives (the "Data Directives") set guidelines for Member States to follow when enacting local data protection legislation. The discussion that follows will cover the principles as a whole and, in some cases, local laws enacted pursuant to the guidelines.

Currently, the Directives are more stringent than privacy laws in the U.S. that focus on regulating data privacy only in discrete categories, such as healthcare and credit records. The Directives, on the other hand, apply to all types of personal information and cover not only electronically collected data but also oral communications.

C. The EU Data Protection Directive Governing Principles

As previously mentioned, the EU Data Protection Directive was designed to safeguard the fundamental rights of consumers, citizens and users of Internet-based services. There are seven primary principles underlying the Directive; the aim of each principle is to require data processors to meet certain criteria before collecting, using or disclosing personal information. These criteria fall into three distinct categories:

1. *Transparency*

This requires that the data subject be informed about how his or her personal information will be collected, stored and used. The "data controller" (discussed further in Chapter Three) is required to provide its contact name and address, disclose the purpose of the processing,[54] identify who will receive the data, and any other information establishing that the processing was initiated fairly.

The Transparency principle emphasizes that personal data can only be processed in the following circumstances:

• *Where consent is freely and explicitly given*

Companies are required to include an "opt-in" choice for individuals whose information they will collect. Data subjects who select the opt-in choice are expressly providing their consent to have their information stored, processed, maintained, or possibly shared with others in the manner described in the privacy policy.

• *To fulfill a legal obligation*

Companies may process personal information to satisfy compliance with a legal obligation.

• *In performance of a contract*

Companies may process personal information when the data is necessary for the performance or creation of a contract.

• *For protection of the Data Subject*

Companies may process personal information when processing is necessary in order to make it possible for the business to protect the vital interests of the Data Subject.

• *In the interest of the public*

Processing of personal information is allowed when necessary for the public's interest or when exercised by official authority.

• *For legitimate interests*

Lastly, processing of personal information is permitted when necessary for legitimate interests, except where the data subject's fundamental interests or rights override the data controller's legitimate interests. An interest will be characterized as "legitimate" if that interest outweighs the fundamental rights and freedoms of the data subject. If there is a dispute as to the legitimacy the Privacy Commissioner may be called upon to make a final determination. There is currently a push by consumer rights groups to require companies to make public the legitimate interest.

**Train Your Staff to Comply
With the GDPR**

Even if you don't think your business is subject to the GDPR provides a helpful "best practices" framework governing processing of personal data. Train your staff to:

✓ Only collect personal data needed for your business' specified purpose.

✓ Keep records accurate and up-to-date.

✓ Promptly notify customers if data will be used in a different manner than that for which they were first collected and get updated consent or provide an opt-out option.

✓ Appropriately dispose of personal data when no longer needed (for details on how to properly discard data, see Chapter Six).

✓ Never release personal data without obtaining authorization from the correct person within your company.

• *Provided that the Data Subject has access to information*

Companies may only process personal information if the data subject has the explicit right to access any or all of his or her personal data that is processed. The data subject also has the right to demand deletion, correction, or blocking of any data that is inaccurate or incomplete, or that is not being processed in compliance with data protection rules.

2. *Legitimate Purpose*.

This category emphasizes that personal data can only be processed for specified, unambiguous and legitimate purposes. The data may not be processed further in a way that is incompatible with specified purposes. A legitimate purpose must be distinguished from the legitimate interest mentioned above. A legitimate purpose should describe the use for which personal information being collected will be made, while the legitimate interest, refers to a disclosure that is outside of the legitimate purpose. For example, personal information is collected for the legitimate purpose of delivering products to a consumer, while a legitimate interest may come into play if that data subject's personal information was requested by a government official, under subpoena, for which failure to comply may result in a contempt citation.

3. *Proportionality*

A data controller may not collect or process personal information if doing so is excessive and not relevant for the indicated purpose. The data must be accurate and reasonable steps must be taken to update or correct the data if they are incomplete or inaccurate. Furthermore, the data controller must take action to delete personal information once the purpose for which it was collected is accomplished. If personal data is kept for statistical or historical purposes, appropriate protection measures must be implemented.

The EU General Data Protection Regulation (GDPR)

After being in place for nearly 20 years the Data Protection Directive will be replaced with an updated and more stringent data privacy regime. The GDPR replaces the Data Protection Directive 95/46/EC and was designed to harmonize data privacy laws across Europe, to protect and empower all EU citizens data privacy and to reshape the way organizations across the region approach data privacy.

After extensive consideration, the GDPR was approved by the EU Parliament on April 14, 2016. The new law will take effect on May 25, 2018 after a two-year transition period and will not require enabling legislation to be passed by national governments. After

May 25, 2018, organizations in non-compliance will face heavy fines.

The GDPR will be the strictest data protection law implemented to date and will be universal in its application. This means that, rather than enacting country-specific laws that followed general principles set out in the Directives, Member States must enact the provisions of the Regulation exactly as written.

"One Stop Shop" Structure

The GDPR represents a simplification of the EU data privacy rules in that now a single set of rules will apply to all EU member states with each member state will establish an independent Supervisory Authority (SA) to hear and investigate complaints and sanction administrative offenses,

From a compliance perspective, businesses that operate from multiple countries will rely on a single SA as its "lead authority." A businesses' lead authority is determined based on the location of its where the main data processing activities take place (main establishment). For example, a business whose operations are in 5 European countries, but conducts its main data processing activities in France would rely on the French SA as its lead authority.

The following represents a summary of the key provisions of the GDPR.

Territorial Scope

The GPDR will apply to the processing of personal data by controllers and processors in the EU, regardless of whether the processing takes place in the EU or not. The GDPR will also apply to the processing of personal data of data subjects in the EU by a controller or processor not established in the EU, where the activities relate to: offering goods or services to EU citizens (irrespective of whether payment is required) and the monitoring of behavior that takes place within the EU. Non-Eu businesses processing the data of EU citizens will also have to appoint a representative in the EU.

Penalties

Organizations that control and process data who violate the GDPR can be fined up to 4% of annual global turnover or €20 Million (whichever is greater) with a tiered fine structure for less serious offenses.

Consent

Companies can no longer use long, complex consent terms, rather it must be given in an intelligible and easily accessible form, with the purpose for data processing attached to that consent.

Breach Notification

Under the GDPR, breach notification will become mandatory in all member states where a data breach is likely to "result in a risk for the rights and freedoms of individuals". Breach notification must be done within 72 hours of first having become aware of the breach. Data processors will also be required to notify their customers, the controllers, "without undue delay" after first becoming aware of a data breach.

Right to Access

Part of the expanded rights of data subjects outlined by the GDPR is the right for data subjects to obtain from the data controller confirmation as to whether or not personal data concerning them is being processed, where and for what purpose. Further, the controller shall provide a copy of the personal data, free of charge, in an electronic format. This change is a dramatic shift to data transparency and empowerment of data subjects.

Data Erasure/Right to be Forgotten

This provision entitles the data subject to have the data controller erase his/her personal data, cease further dissemination of the data, and potentially have third parties halt processing of the data.

Data Portability

The GDPR establishes the right for a data subject to receive the personal data concerning them, which they have previously provided in a 'commonly use and machine-readable format' and have the right to transmit that data to another controller.

Privacy by Design

Under the GDPR calls for the inclusion of data protection from the onset of the designing of systems, rather than an addition.

Data Minimization

The GDPR calls for controllers to hold and process only the data absolutely necessary for the completion of its duties (data minimization), as well as limiting the access to personal data to those needing to act out the processing.

Data Protection Officers

Under GDPR it will not be necessary to submit notifications / registrations to each local DPA of data processing activities, nor will it be a requirement to notify / obtain approval for transfers based on the Model Contract Clauses (MCCs). Instead, there will be internal record keeping requirements, as further explained below, and DPO appointment will be mandatory only for those controllers and processors whose core activities consist of processing operations which require regular and systematic monitoring of data subjects on a large scale or of special categories of data or data relating to criminal convictions and offences.

Data Transfers Outside the EU

The GDPR's provisions relating to international transfers of personal data is similar to the existing regime under the Directives. The Directive prohibits transfers of personal data outside of EU Member States unless the country in which the data is received has enacted adequate data protection safeguards. In some cases, companies may have to seek permission from the national data protection authority before transferring any data outside the EU.

Companies located in the EU, or doing business in the EU, will continue to deal with over 27 different national data protection laws until implementation of the proposed Regulation. The fragmentary nature of the locally-implemented laws is proving to be a costly administrative burden that made it difficult for businesses to access new markets or guarantee complete data protection for each customer.[55] The resources needed to ensure compliance are significant, as are the fines for noncompliance.

What is a Cross-Border Data Transfer?

A cross-border data transfer occurs when a business transfers customer information across the border of a consumer's country to a server located in another country, even if it's for a brief period of time. Such data transfers are often a necessary requirement for businesses: data servers, for example, are frequently located in low-tax or offshore jurisdictions, and third-party vendors also frequently choose to locate in countries where the vendor can operate in the most cost-effective and efficient manner possible, automatic data backups can also be made to servers in different countries as part of a global security plan. Thanks to modern technology, cross-border data transfers may occur instantaneously. While this may be an essential and convenient feature of online business, cross-border data transfers also increase the risk of unintentional disclosure.

If You Have Customers in EU Member States, Can You Transfer Their Personal Information Out of the EU?

The prohibition on transferring personal data outside of the EU unless the receiving country's laws provide "adequate protection" can be overcome if you provide customers with notice about what you plan to do with their data and you get customers' informed consent.

What constitutes adequate "notice" and "consent" varies from country to country, but one of the most important considerations is **using an opt-in agreement** for consent to cross-border data transfers.

D. Examples of Data Protection Legislation Enacted Based on the Data Protection Directive's Principles

Following are examples of laws passed by EU Member States based on the 1995 Data Protection Directive. As you will notice, the laws share common characteristics but, at the same time, there are differences that pose challenges for companies doing business in more than one of these countries. Further, this section will note any potential changes in these laws in light of the passage of the GDPR.

United Kingdom: Data Protection Act 1998

The Data Protection Act 1998[56] ("DPA") is the UK's implementation of the principles set out in the EU Data Protection Directive. Enforcement of the DPA is done through the Information Commissioner's Office ("ICO"), and data processors are required to inform the ICO prior to processing personal data, so that their processing may be registered and publicized in the Register of Data Controllers (unless an exemption applies).

Under the UK's DPA, collection, processing and transfer of personal information must meet any one of a number of requirements before any of these activities takes places. These requirements are nearly identical to those detailed under the EU Data Protection Directive and the GDPR. They state that, in order to collect or process personal information, a company must obtain the data subject's consent; it must be necessary in order to carry out a contract where the subject is a party; or, it must be required to satisfy the data collector's legal obligations or to protect its vital interests. Moreover, the data controller must have a legitimate purpose for processing the information. Transfers of personal information outside of Europe are subject to similar restrictions.

Lastly, it is important to note that the GDPR will apply in the UK upon its enforcement date on May 25, 2018. The government confirms that the UK's decision to leave the EU will not affect the commencement of the GDPR. Therefore, when conducting data collection and processing operations in the UK it is important to understand the obligations incumbent under the GDPR and the DPA.

Germany: Federal Data Protection Act (Bundesdatenschutzgesetz)

Germany's law implementing the EU Data Protection Directive is known as the Federal Data Protection Act (*Bundesdatenschutzgesetz* in German).[57] In addition, each of Germany's 16 states has enacted data protection legislation. Enforcement of data protection is primarily done at the state level. In contrast with data protection laws in most other EU Member States, Germany does not require data controllers to register before processing personal data. The Act, like the UK's DPA, requires notification when data controllers collect or process personal information. This condition does not apply, however, if the data controller has appointed a DPO. Companies with over nine people engaged in automatic processing of personal information must appoint a DPO. Lastly, under Germany's Act, unlike the UK's DPA, data controllers must notify data subjects in certain circumstances if there has been a breach of personal information.

Recently, the High Court of Berlin had an opportunity to review a case brought against Facebook by the Federation of German Consumer Organizations, in which the group claimed that Facebook was in breach of the Federal Data Protection Act, by sending emails to non-users without their consent through use of the "Friend Finder" feature. The High Court placed particular importance on the use of cookies, holding that Facebook, as a data controller, used "equipment" in Germany when it placed cookies on the devices of German users, regardless of whether they were Facebook users. This is significant since Facebook, a U.S. company, argued that any German data was controlled and processed from its operations in

Ireland and, therefore, Irish data protection laws applied. Yet the High Court held that Facebook did not provide sufficient evidence to demonstrate that its Irish operations actually made the decisions expected from a data controller, rather the U.S. operations were deemed the decision maker. This is the first such examination and determination, and will likely be followed by other Member States.

On April 27, 2017, the German Parliament passed an entirely new Federal Data Protection Act. The new law adapts German data privacy law to the provisions of **GDPR**.

The Netherlands: Dutch Personal Data Protection Act

The Netherlands enacted the principles of the EU Data Protection Data in 2001 with the Dutch Personal Data Protection Act.[58] The Dutch Data Protection Authority "***Autoriteit Persoonsgegevens***". is responsible for enforcing the Act. Companies that process personal data through automatic means must register with the CBP, and notification is required, before commencing data processing.

The Law on Data Breach Notifications (*Wet Meldplicht datalekken en uitbreiding bestuurlijke boetebevoegdheid Cbp*) ("**Breach Notification Law**") came into force on 1 January 2016. Under the new law, data controllers are required to provide notification of any data breach: to the DPA if such breach has serious adverse consequences for the protection of personal data; and to affected individuals to the extent the breach is likely to have unfavorable consequences for the privacy of these individuals. However, if the personal data is encrypted a notification is not required. Lastly, data controllers are also required to address data breaches in their contractual relationship with data processors.

E. Does Having a Data Protection Officer Help with Compliance?

Now that we have familiarized ourselves with the EU Data Directives, which represent some of the most influential data protection legislation worldwide, it is useful to briefly revisit the concept of a DPO. The GDPR will effectively replace all locally-enacted data protection laws, and will require companies to appoint a DPO, and that some jurisdictions—such as Germany—already obligate companies over a certain size to do so.

The rapidly evolving nature of data protection laws makes it a likelihood that your business, whether located in the EU or not, would be required by law to appoint a DPO in the not-too-distant future. Even if not required by law, a DPO is still an essential component of effective data privacy and protection at your company. Not only will that individual help understand the nature of complex legal regimes, such as the one that currently exists in the EU, but also the DPO will lead the development and ensure accountability in a privacy protection program at your company.

The Data Protection Officer typically will:

✓ Develop and draft the data privacy program and policy

✓ Train all internal staff and ensure training is completed

✓ Take responsibility for periodic assessment and make changes as necessary to maintain compliance with any applicable laws

✓ Respond to inquiries regarding the company's privacy policies

✓ Process requests and complaints

DPO Obligations under the GDPR

Under the GDPR, some private sector and most public sector organizations are required to appoint a DPO. Private-sector organizations engaged in operations that involve data controlling and processing must designate a DPO if their core activities involve:

1. operations which, by virtue of their nature, their scope and/or their purposes, require regular and systematic monitoring of data subjects on a large scale or

2. processing on a large scale of special categories of data and data relating to criminal convictions and offences.

All public authorities or bodies, except courts acting in their judicial capacity, must designate a DPO.[59]

References

[49] Council Directive CETS No. 108, 1981, *available at* http://conventions.coe.int/Treaty/en/Treaties/Html/108.htm

[50] Treaty on the Functioning of the European Union art. 16, 2010 O.J. (C 83) 47, *available at* http://www.lisbon-treaty.org/wcm/the-lisbon-treaty/treaty-on-the-functioning-of-the-european-union-and-comments/part-1-principles/title-ii-provisions-having-general-application/158-article-16.html

[51] *Available at* http://www.echr.coe.int/Documents/Convention_ENG.pdf (last visited Feb. 6, 2014).

[52] Council Directive 2000/C 364/01, *available at* http://www.europarl.europa.eu/charter/pdf/text_en.pdf

[53] 2000 O.J. (L 8/1), *available at* eurlex.europa.eu/LexUriServ/LexUriServ.do?uri=OJ:L:2001:008:0001:0022:en:PDF

[54] Defined in Article 2(b) of the Directive: ***processing*** means "any operation or set of operations which is performed upon personal data, whether or not by automatic means, such as collection, recording, organization, storage, adaptation or alteration, retrieval, consultation, use, disclosure by transmission,

dissemination or otherwise making available, alignment or combination, blocking, erasure or destruction."

[55] Google, for example, has been the target of enforcement action by France, Germany, Italy, Spain, the Netherlands and the UK for allegedly violating the Data Protection Directive. Farah Coppola, *EU Enforcement Action Against Google*, EUROPEAN PUB. AFFAIRS (Apr. 15, 2013), http://www.europeanpublicaffairs.eu/eu-enforcement-action-against-google/

[56] UK Data Protection Act 1998 available at http://www.legislation.gov.uk/ukpga/1998/29/contents

[57] Federal Data Protection Act available at https://www.gesetze-im-Internet.de/englisch_bdsg/englisch_bdsg.html

[58] Dutch Personal Data Protection Act (2001) available at https://www.akd.nl/t/Documents/17-03-2016_ENG_Wet-bescherming-persoonsgegevens.pdf

[59] EU general data protection regulation 2016/679 Art. 37 available at https://www.privacy-regulation.eu/en/37.htm

CHAPTER FOUR - REGIONAL TRENDS AND MULTIJURISDICTIONAL CONFLICTS

A. Regional Trends

Australia

Similar to the U.S. system, data protection in Australia is regulated by an assortment of federal and state/territorial laws. The most significant piece of legislation governing the handling of individuals' personal information is the Australian Privacy Act 1988 ("Privacy Act").[60] The Privacy Act consists of two sets of principles applicable to the collection, use, storage, and disclosure of personal information: one applicable to public entities, and one applicable to private entities.

Public-sector entities are charged with following the 11 Information Privacy Principles, which regulate things such as the manner and purpose of personal data collection, storage and security, and how individuals may access or amend data about themselves.

Private organizations must generally comply with the Privacy Act's 10 National Privacy Principles. These principles regulate personal data handling in much the same way as public-sector entities, but include provisions requiring businesses to let individuals remain anonymous, if possible, and regulating trans-border data flows.

Australian states and territories (except for the states of Western Australia and South Australia) each have enacted data privacy laws applicable to the state government's agencies and private organizations' interactions with those agencies. These laws are:

• The Information Act 2002 (Northern Territory);[61]

- The Privacy and Personal Information Protection Act 1998 (New South Wales);[62]

- The Information Privacy Act 2009 (Queensland);[63]

- The Personal Information and Protection Act 2004 (Tasmania);[64] and

- The Information Privacy Act 2000 (Victoria).[65]

Private Amendment (Enhancing Privacy Protection) Act 2012[66]: In November 2012, the Australian Parliament passed significant amendments to the Commonwealth's Privacy Act that went into effect on March 12, 2014. Among other things, the revisions include one set of 13 principles applicable to both public and private entities and increased enforcement powers for the Australian Information Commissioner.

Comparison with the EU Data Directive and the GDPR: Despite undergoing amendment in 2000 and 2004, the Australian Privacy Act has not been deemed to provide "adequate protection" to personal data under the EU Directive, and thus transfer of personal information between EU member countries and Australian businesses is (theoretically) restricted. In practice, though, many Australian companies continue doing business with EU member nations by inserting the relevant privacy standards in contracts between the parties. Two significant differences between the EU Directive and Australia's Privacy Act include the fact that, unlike the EU, Australia's government does not maintain a database recording "controllers of processing activities." Also dissimilar from the EU, organizations are not required to report personal data processing information to the Australian Information Commissioner.

Africa

South Africa

South Africa has, in the recent past, had the dubious distinction of being named the worst country for data privacy protection in the cloud out of 24 countries evaluated. Although the Republic of South Africa Constitution generally guarantees the right to privacy, the country does not currently have any laws in place providing for protection of personal data. South Africa does have an Electronic Communications and Transaction Act in place that provides for some regulations governing collection of personal information. However, businesses are not required by law to comply with these provisions of the Act; instead, their compliance is voluntary.

South Africa's reputation for a lack of privacy protections is about to change, however, because in November 2013, the country's Parliament signed the new Protection of Personal Information Act ("POPI")[67] into law. Among other reforms, POPI establishes an independent statutory body, the Office of Information Regulator, to promote the goals of the Act through education and research as well as auditing organizations for compliance, mediation of disputes, and investigation of complaints. POPI will require both public and private organizations to report to the new Office of Information Regulator before processing personal information. The Regulator will maintain a database of which organizations have processed personal information and for what purpose. Individuals may request to access their information in these records free of charge. One of the most stringent requirements of POPI is that an individual must consent before an organization is allowed to transfer his or her information out of the country (to third-party cloud providers, for example).

Comparison with the EU Data Directive and the GDPR: In August 2013, the EU began requiring telecommunications operators and

Internet Service Providers ("ISP") to report any theft, loss, or unauthorized access to personal information to the appropriate national authorities. Similarly, in the proposed comprehensive reform of the EU Data Directive that is not yet in force, one new proposal requires organizations to report "serious data breaches" to national authorities within 24 hours. South Africa's new POPI Act also, orders organizations to notify the Office of Information Regulator of potential breaches involving personal information. Unlike the EU, however, South Africa requires the responsible party to notify the individuals whose information was comprised as well.

Asia

China

China does not currently have a comprehensive system of laws in place that regulates data privacy. However, China is moving towards putting such a system in place.

In December 2012, the Standing Committee of the Chinese National People's Congress announced a Decision on Strengthening the Protection of Online Information. The Decision applies to both public and private entities and governs personal information on the Internet and should be treated as enforceable law.

Soon after China released its Decision, in January 2013 its Ministry of Industry and Information Technology Standardization Administration released the Information Security Technology – Guidelines for Personal Information Protection Within Public and Commercial Services Information Systems. The guidelines apply to a broader range of businesses than the 2012 Decision and cover some areas left open in the earlier document. While the guidelines are voluntary and lack the force of law, they do show China's increased commitment to regulating personal data.

A draft Personal Data Protection Law has been under consideration by the PRC Government for many years, however there is no indication as to if and when such law will be passed.

India

India does not have any laws in place specifically providing for the regulation of personal information. India's Information Technology Act ("IT Act"), originally passed in 2000, was later amended to include Sections 43A and 72A, both of which give individuals the right to be compensated if their personal information is improperly disclosed. A new set of rules was issued under the IT Act Section 43A in 2011 that imposed new obligations on private organizations India that engage in collection or disclosure of data. India's Ministry of Communications and Information subsequently issued a "Press Note" later that year, clarifying that Indian outsourcing service providers (organizations that collect, store, or handle personal information) contracting with clients inside or outside of India are not subject to the collection and disclosure of information requirements if they do not have direct contact with the individuals whose information they collect, store, or handle.

Japan

Japan is considered by many to have very robust laws protecting personal information. The most significant law in this area is the Act on the Protection of Personal Information ("APPI")[68], which was passed in 2003 and came into force in 2005. The APPI requires organizations that handle information to conform to a number of requirements, including:

• Specifying the purpose for collecting and processing personal information;

• Refraining from changing that purpose too far from the originally stated purpose;

• Only processing personal information to the extent required to achieve the stated purpose unless new consent is obtained from the individual; and

• Obtaining the consent of the individual data subject if the organization receives the information as a result of "succession" from another business (e.g., purchase of another business) if the information will be used in a manner different from the originally stated purpose.

Amendments to the APPI[69], were passed in 2015 and went into effect on May 30, 2017 apply the APPI to all businesses in Japan, regardless of whether the business operator maintains a database of more than 5,000 individuals. The Amendments, further clarify the definition of personal information, add two new classes of information, and introduce new requirements for "opt out" choice for business operators to disclosure personal information to third parties. Finally, the Amendments created a Privacy Protection Commission (the "Commission"), a central agency which will act as a supervisory governmental organization on issues of privacy protection.

Comparison with the EU Data Protection Directive and GDPR: Japan's APPI is similar to the EU Data Protection Directive in that Japan requires entities to obtain individual consent prior to sharing personal information with third parties, including affiliated companies. Unlike the EU, Japan does not distinguish between transfers of information outside the country and those that take place within. Even those transfers of information that take place inside Japan to third parties, therefore, require consent from the individual.

Eastern Europe

Russia

Fundamental respect for privacy of individuals' data and principles to protect that data in Russia come from the Convention for the Protection of Individuals with regard to Automatic Processing of Personal Data ("Convention"). First adopted by the Council of Europe in 1981, the Convention sets out legally binding standards for the protection of personal data, implementing Articles 8 and 10 of the European Convention for the Protection of Human Rights, specifically obliges participating Parties to the Convention to adhere to the principles of fairness, legality, proportionality, adequacy, accuracy, confidentiality and notification of data subjects. This Convention, initially ratified by the Russian Federation in 2005 and most recently in September 2013, created standards applicable to all parties engaged in data processing, by making changes to 14 laws, including the Labor Code, the Civil Procedure Code, federal laws on the Prosecutor's Office, on acts of civil status, on non-State pension funds, on the welfare state, on the state bank of data on children without parental care, on the communication, on lotteries and others.

The year after Russia adopted the Convention, the country's Federal Law on Personal Data (No. 152-FZ) ("Personal Data Protection Act") came into force. The Personal Data Protection Act requires "data operators" to obtain written consent from the regulatory body charged with compliance, "Roscomnadzor," before the data operators may process personal information, unless an exemption applies. The Personal Data Act also generally mandates individual consent before personal data about that person may be collected or processed, except when necessary to perform a contract and the individual is a party to that contract. In July 2011, the Personal Data Protection Act was amended significantly to broaden the definition of personal data that should be protected and required data operators to appoint responsible employees for processing of personal data, develop standard procedures for processing personal data, and audit compliance with those procedures.

In 2012, two new government regulations were signed:

1. Regulation n 211 (dated 21.03.2012) stating the list of measures and standard forms to be used by operators for documenting the fulfillment of their responsibilities under the Personal Data Act.

2. Regulation n 1119 (dated 01.11.2012) stating technical security requirements for personal data when processing in operational systems, defining four levels of protection of such data, corresponding to the security risk of specific data items.

Roscomnadzor has increased its vigilance in light of these new rules, with audits and sanctions doubling in 2013 compared to 2011.

If a foreign company has a website not registered in the .ru or .рф top-level domains, Russian laws are not applicable. However, Roscomnadzor enforces international laws and regularly contacts their counterparts in other countries in order to protect the personal data of Russian citizens, requesting the deletion of unprotected personal data about Russian citizens and even requesting closure of websites which do not respect personal data protection law.

In 2014 the Personal Data Protection Act was further amended to require all personal data operators to store and process any personal data of Russian individuals within databases located in Russia and an enhanced penalty provision for data mishandling which allows for the blocking of websites involving unlawful handling of Russian personal data. Further, the amendments allows for the creation of a Register of Infringers of Rights of Personal Data Subjects by the Roscomnadzor.

Comparison with the EU Data Protection Directive and GDPR:
Russia, like the EU, requires a party who wishes to transfer personal data out of the country to ensure that the country receiving the transfer provides the data with an adequate level of protection. Any nation that has ratified the Convention is deemed to provide sufficient protection for purposes of the Personal Data Act.

South America

Argentina

In Argentina, the right to protection of personal information is written into the national constitution. Under section 43 of the Constitution of the Argentine Nation, individuals have the right to access information about themselves contained in public and private databases. Moreover, individuals may request amendment or updating of their personal information, ask for confidentiality, or demand the information be withheld from disclosure or use if it is incorrect.

In addition to the protections afforded by the constitution, the Data Protection Act of Argentina, Law 25,326 ("DPA")[70] came into effect in November 2000. The DPA, modeled after Spain's data protection law, requires "data users" (owners of databases of personal data) to get consent from "data owners" to collect personal information and to disclose the purpose of the data collection, except in certain circumstances. Data users must register annually with the "Directorate," the regulatory body overseeing data protection in Argentina.

Like the EU, Argentina prohibits the transfer of personal information outside the country to nations that do not have laws providing "adequate protection" to private data. As far back as 2003, the EU has recognized Argentina as a nation with laws providing an adequate level of protection under the EU Data Protection Directive, so organizations in either jurisdiction are free to transfer personal information between themselves without further action.

In early 2017 the Argentina Data Protection Agency posted a draft copy of a new data protection act. The draft bill based heavily on the EU GDPR.

Brazil

Like several other countries, Brazil's constitution contains general principles relating to privacy rights and data protection. Brazil does not, however, have any specific legislation governing data protection, and organizations that collect personal information about individuals are not required to obtain consent before collecting the information. Some industry-specific laws (relating to finance, healthcare, and telecommunications, for example) do impose certain data privacy restrictions on organizations.

Brazil's lack of a comprehensive law regulating data privacy was the primary reason it was ranked at the bottom of a list of 24 countries in terms of its readiness to support cloud computing, as measured in terms of several measures like its ability to ensure privacy, promote security, and battle cybercrime.[71]

The Brazilian Internet Act[72] establishes a limited set of obligations concerning the storage and use of data collected online.

Further, there are two bills (No. 330/2013 and No. 5.276/2016), under consideration by the Congress that address data privacy.

B. Multijurisdictional Conflicts in Data Privacy Laws

Introduction: Jurisdiction and Conflicts of Laws in Cyberspace

With so many data privacy laws in effect across the globe and with so many companies transmitting personal data over the Internet, it is not surprising for companies of any size today to find themselves subject to the data privacy laws of both their own country and any number of other jurisdictions.

Given the inconsistency in data privacy laws worldwide, it is possible (if not likely) that a company might be subject to two or more laws that are in conflict with one another. This conflict creates two related issues: (1) knowing *where* your organization might be brought to court in the event of an allegation of mishandling of personal data and (2) knowing *which country's* law will govern (or, in other words, knowing which country's laws your organization should be following).

Knowing Where You Might be Brought Into Court (Jurisdiction)

If an organization is subject to the data privacy laws of its own country and several other nations—because it is an online retailer that accepts orders from, and collects data about, customers worldwide, for example—the organization may potentially be sued in its own country and the country of any of its customers, suppliers, or third-party data processors. That is, a court in any of those places may exercise jurisdiction over the organization.

Example 1. A U.S.-Based Company Collects Information from a UK Citizen: Suppose a company headquartered in the U.S. provides virus protection software for computers. A UK citizen downloads the software for his computer, filling out a form with his personal data (name, address, and credit card information for payment). Later, the UK citizen learns that the database containing his personal information was hacked and sues the software company in the UK and under UK data privacy law for mishandling information. May the U.S. company be sued in a UK court?

It is likely that the U.S. company could be brought into court in the UK. Like U.S. courts, the UK courts look at a variety of factors to determine whether a case should be allowed to go forward there, including the amount of contacts the company has with that jurisdiction and the fairness of allowing the company to be sued there. In early 2014, a UK court announced that a small group of individuals could continue a suit against Google alleging the Internet giant "tricked" Apple's Safari web browser into accepting Google's tracking cookies even when users set their browsers to refuse the cookies. According to the judge, allowing the lawsuit to continue in the UK was appropriate "because it dealt with a 'developing area' of English law, and because it was unreasonable to expect a small group of individuals to spend a fortune suing Google in the U.S. when the alleged damage was done in England."[73]

It is possible that, if the U.S.-based company has never had an order from a UK citizen before the one in this example and the company neither targets nor advertises to UK citizens, a court in the UK would not allow the lawsuit to go forward there. Again, this determination would be based on the consideration of factors such as the amount of contact with the country (here, there is almost none) and the fairness of bringing the U.S. company into court in the UK (it seems much less fair to make a retailer who has only had one order from a UK customer defend itself in a UK court).

Example 2. A U.S.-Based Company Uses Cloud Computing: It may seem intuitive to say that an individual claiming he was harmed by a company's mishandling of his personal information should be able to sue that company in the individual's home country. However, what if the company uses a third party located in a different country to store its data, and the third party mishandles the data?

Using the software or hardware of a third party located in a remote location, known as cloud computing, makes it difficult to know where the "harm" to an individual occurred and thus where a company may be sued. The general consensus is that a company may be sued in the jurisdiction where a third-party provider is located, in addition to the company's home country and the country where the individual bringing the suit is located. For that reason, companies using the "cloud" should know at a minimum where their service provider is located and the location of its data servers, as well as the amount of revenue produced by each location. The amount of revenue is important in establishing the extent of the company's operations in a given jurisdiction.

Knowing Which Country's Law Might Govern (Choice of Law)

Once a court exercises jurisdiction over the organization, that does not mean the laws of that country automatically apply. Which country's laws do apply is significant because an organization might be found liable under one country's (stricter) data privacy laws and not liable under another country's (more lenient) laws. How a court decides which law to apply is referred to as a *choice of law* decision. Consider two scenarios that might arise in international cyberspace:

Example 3. The U.S.-Based Company's Privacy Policy Specifies New York Law Will Govern: Continuing with Example 1 above and the U.S.-based antivirus software provider, assume the U.S.-based organization requires customers to agree to the terms of its data privacy policy by clicking on "I agree" at the bottom of a web page displaying its policy. Customers must agree to the terms of the policy before downloading the antivirus software. What if the policy specifies that, in the event of a disagreement, New York law will apply?

The answer to this question would not be found in the data privacy laws of the U.S. or the country where the customer is located.

Instead, companies will need to look to contract law to understand how courts might treat provisions like this one, because the data privacy policy establishes a contract between the company and the customer. Provisions in a contract like the one in this example are generally found to be binding under U.S., Canadian, and UK law. Thus, it is likely that a court in any of these countries would apply New York law, as the data privacy policy asks it to.

A court in an EU member country might also think a contract provision like this one would be valid, although this is less certain. Whether the court would uphold an agreement like this would be determined by looking to the applicable international law, which would depend on specific circumstances such as where the parties are located and what their relationship is (buyer and seller of goods, for example). If the parties were located in two EU Member States (or an EU Member State and a non-EU member), the court would look to the Rome I Regulation, a directive passed by the European Commission that tells courts which law governs in cases involving international contracts. Under the Rome I Regulation, courts are told that provisions in the contract like the New York choice-of-law provision should generally be respected.

If a private business in one country sells goods to a private business located in another country, that relationship is governed by the United Nations Convention on Contracts for the International Sale of Goods ("CISG"). Over 80 countries, including the U.S., Canada and several EU Member States (but excluding the UK) have adopted this treaty. Under the CISG, contract provisions specifying which law to apply in a dispute are valid if the contract expressly states that the contract's choice-of-law provision, rather than the CISG default rules, apply.

Example 4. A UK-Based Company Has an Arbitration Clause in its Website Terms and Conditions: Suppose a UK-based online retailer includes the following language in the terms and conditions: "All claims and disputes arising under or relating to this Agreement are to be settled by binding arbitration in the city of London, England." Will a court respect this agreement?

Companies doing business over the Internet often include arbitration agreements in the terms and conditions they post on their site. Such provisions state that, instead of (or in addition to) having a provision specifying which country's law will apply, the parties agree to undergo arbitration—a less expensive process than a lawsuit, but which cannot generally be appealed to a higher authority—in the event of a dispute. International arbitration agreements in many countries are regulated by the Convention on the Recognition and Enforcement of Foreign Arbitral Awards (also known as the "New York Convention"). This treaty, which has been adopted by 146 United Nations member states, states that members shall recognize international arbitration agreements and enforce international arbitration awards.

References

[60] Privacy Act 1988 available at
http://www.austlii.edu.au/au/legis/cth/consol_act/pa1988108/

[61]   The   Information   Act   2002   available   at
http://www.austlii.edu.au/au/legis/nt/consol_act/ia144/

[62] The Privacy and Personal Information Protection Act 1998 available at
http://www.legislation.nsw.gov.au/#/view/act/1998/133

[63]   The   Information   Privacy   Act   2009   available   at
https://www.legislation.qld.gov.au/LEGISLTN/CURRENT/I/InfoPrivA09.pdf

[64] The Personal Information and Protection Act 2004 available at
http://www.austlii.edu.au/au/legis/tas/consol_act/pipa2004361/

[65]   The   Information   Privacy   Act   (2000)   available   at
http://www.legislation.vic.gov.au/Domino/Web_Notes/LDMS/PubStatbook.nsf/
f932b66241ecf1b7ca256e92000e23be/4BE13AE4A4C3973ECA256E5B00213F
50/$FILE/00-098a.pdf

[66] Private Amendment (Enhancing Privacy Protection) Act 2012 available at
https://www.legislation.gov.au/Details/C2012A00197

[67] Protection of Personal Information Act (2013) available at http://www.gov.za/sites/www.gov.za/files/37067_26-11_Act4of2013ProtectionOfPersonalInfor_correct.pdf

[68] Act on the Protection of Personal Information Act No. 57 of (2003) available at http://www.cas.go.jp/jp/seisaku/hourei/data/APPI.pdf

[69] Amended Act on the Protection of Personal Information available at https://www.ppc.go.jp/files/pdf/Act_on_the_Protection_of_Personal_Infomration.pdf

[70] Data Protection Act of Argentina, available at http://unpan1.un.org/intradoc/groups/public/documents/un-dpadm/unpan044147.pdf

[71]   BSA   Global   Cloud   Computing   Scorecard, http://cloudscorecard.bsa.org/2013/index.html

[72] Marco Civil Law of the Internet in Brazil available at https://www.cgi.br/pagina/marco-civil-law-of-the-Internet-in-brazil/180

[73] David Meyer, *Privacy Activists Can Sue Google in UK Over Safari Tracking, Court Decides*, GIGAOM, http://gigaom.com/2014/01/16/privacy-activists-can-sue-google-in-uk-over-safari-tracking-court-decides/ (last visited Jan. 24, 2014)

CHAPTER FIVE – OUTSOURCING

A. Introduction

Thus far, we have visited a number of important issues falling under the general umbrella of data privacy and protection including drafting of a privacy policy, exploration of data privacy laws in some of the major world economies, and understanding multijurisdictional conflicts in data privacy laws. This chapter aims to discuss some of the data privacy issues that arise in the context of outsourcing and, with those issues in mind, to provide practical advice on handling personal data within your business—from developing a breach incident response plan, to training your staff to properly handle personal data, to data retention and disposal best practices. This chapter additionally covers some examples of private and regulatory enforcement actions for breach of data privacy laws, in order to help you better appreciate the variety of legal proceedings that might be brought against companies for non-compliance.

B. Use of a Cloud Service Provider to Collect, Store and Transfer Information

As has been mentioned elsewhere in this book, cloud computing refers to the practice of storing and accessing data through the Internet, rather than your computer's hard drive. *PC Magazine* has noted that "the cloud is just a metaphor for the Internet."[74] Companies using Dropbox for online storage, Google Drive for file sharing or online document editing, or PayPal for payment services are all engaging in cloud computing. And cloud computing goes far beyond just these examples: a recent survey by IBM and the Economist Intelligence Unit revealed that about two-thirds of companies with revenues less than USD$1 billion engage in cloud computing in one form or another.

One of the main advantages of cloud computing is that it saves cost on IT infrastructure: instead of buying more memory for a hard drive or software programs to install onto your employees' computers, for example, you are paying to "rent" software that is stored on outside vendors' machines. Cloud computing also allows for increased flexibility—to access files from multiple devices, for example—and "scalability"—a benefit that includes the ability to easily and quickly add new users to a system.

Despite its many advantages, cloud computing also presents drawbacks. One of the most significant downsides is the possibility that your company may be held liable for a third-party vendor's breach of your customer's personal data. Your third-party vendor may intentionally mishandle your customers' private data. A more likely scenario, though, is that an unintentional data breach occurs: something as simple as the loss of a thumb drive at your third-party vendor's premises that contains personal customer information, for example, or as malicious as an intentional hacking of your vendor's databases.

The most fail-proof way to minimize liability associated with third-party vendors would be to include, in your company's service contract with that vendor, a provision requiring the vendor to represent and warrant that they comply with applicable laws and regulations. There are two problems with this, however. First, as seen in Chapter Four of this book, it is not always clear which country's data privacy laws will apply to your company and, likewise, which laws apply to your third-party vendors. Second, most SMEs contract with relatively large third-party vendors such as Amazon, Microsoft, and Google, each with their own set of standard service agreements which they are unlikely to open for negotiation.

So how should you maintain safety in the cloud? For starters, thoroughly read the contracts with any third-party providers to understand (1) where your provider is located, (2) where your data is being stored (because the servers may be in a locale separate from your provider's business), and (3) what security measures your provider takes to keep your customers' data safe. If any of your vendors, or the servers where the data are stored, are in a country with notably lax data protection laws (developed economies are generally considered to have more robust data privacy controls), you should strongly consider searching for a new provider. For example, a number of less developed countries also host a significant amount of remote data services. Less developed countries such as Brazil, India, Pakistan, Indonesia, Philippines, and Turkey, who host a large proportion of these services also have poor data protections in place.[75] As such, you should understand how your provider is protecting customer information through use of appropriate software and infrastructure testing and control. Finally, you should know which country's data privacy law your vendor is following and how it is meeting those constraints.

C. Data Breach Insurance

The rising cost of data breaches is spawning a new underwriting market: data breach insurance. While comprehensive general liability ("CGL") insurance policies may provide some relief in the event of a data breach, there are often strict exclusions for electronic data. CGL policies that provide coverage for third-party claims for personal injury where "personal injury" is defined broadly enough to include oral and written publication that violates a person's right to privacy, may respond to cover data breach claims. However, most CGL policies will specifically exclude claims, whether first-party or third-party, for data breaches.

In 2011, Sony's PlayStation Network was hacked and exposed information on 100 million users.[76] The estimated cost to Sony in that fiscal year alone was $178 million[77], only a small portion of which would be covered by insurance. Target's recent breach, by recent estimates puts its costs related to data breach at over $61 million, only $44 million is covered by insurance.

The costs and expenses arising from a data breach can include:

- Notifying customers

- Credit monitoring

- Lawsuits brought by data subjects whose information was disclosed

- Regulatory action

- Recovery or restoration of lost data

- Loss of reputation and goodwill

- Lost profits

Insurance companies are now offering specialty policies including Information Privacy and Security Insurance and Data Privacy Insurance, although depending on the company might be known as Cyber/Data Breach Insurance, and each can be tailored to your company's needs. With these standalone policies, it is important to know what is covered and what is excluded from the coverage. Are there sub-limits that apply to certain types of data breaches. Premiums can be extremely expensive with some insurance companies requiring data security systems, policies and procedures to be in compliance with SSAE[78]16 standards which goes beyond the previous SAS 70 standard by not only verifying the controls and processes, but also requiring a written assertion regarding the design and operating effectiveness of the controls being reviewed.

Most insurances companies will offer a free risk assessment before binding insurance coverage. Armed with information from the risk assessment, change your data privacy policy or the systems used to address weaknesses. Obtain multiple quotes for a standalone policy or check with your current insurer to determine whether data breach coverage can be included in your CGL policy.

References

[74] Eric Griffith, *What is Cloud Computing?*, PCMAG (Mar. 13, 2013), http://www.pcmag.com/article2/0,2817,2372163,00.asp.

[75] Dlapiperdataprotection.com. (2017). DLA Piper Global Data Protection Laws of the World - World Map. online Available at: https://www.dlapiperdataprotection.com/ Accessed 1 Jul. 2017.

[76] International Insurance News, *Zurich Seeks to Clarify Insurance Coverage of Sony Hack Attack,* July 25, 2011.

[77] *Id.*

[78] Statement on Standards for Attestation Engagements, developed by the Auditing Standards Board of the American Institute of Certified Public Accountants.

CHAPTER SIX – RESPONDING TO AN INCIDENT

**Tips to Minimize Your Chance of a
Data Breach Incident**

✓ Use strong passwords (a mix of alpha and numeric characters as well as upper- and lowercase letters; use symbols; use non-conventional spellings) and require account users to regularly update passwords.

✓ Safeguard access to your network using virtual private network ("VPN") connections, encoded web communications such as SSL and https, and secure wireless networks.

✓ Keep wireless devices and all software current and up-to-date.

✓ Have a plan for handling lost wireless devices, such as remote wipe (allowing you to remotely delete data from a device), auto wipe (providing for data deletion after a number of failed login attempts to a device), or geofencing (providing for data deletion after a device is taken outside a defined physical boundary).

✓ Develop a comprehensive data protection strategy which includes how customers will be notified in the event of an incident.

A. Incidence Response Timing and Process

Now that you are becoming more familiar with how different countries provide for the protection of personal information and the importance of data privacy protection, some more practical information is in order.

Specifically, what should you do if you discover that your customers' personal information has been compromised—who would you notify first and what remedial measures would you take?

As a primary matter, you should know how data breaches could occur so you can take proactive steps to prevent them. In addition to that, you should have a process in place for notifying the appropriate authorities and taking corrective action if a breach does take place. Finally, you should consider the breach from a marketing perspective—do you notify your clients, customers, or suppliers of the incident even if not required by law, and if so, how do you make them comfortable with continuing to do business with you? Each of these is considered in turn.

When considering data breaches, many people assume they are caused by intentional theft—perhaps by hackers—of personal information. In fact, one 2015 survey states, human error represents 52 percent of the root cause of security breaches, according to a CompTIA, survey of individuals from hundreds of companies in the U.S.

Asked about the top examples of human error, 42 percent of those surveyed cited "end user failure to follow policies and procedures," another 42 percent cited "general carelessness," 31 percent named "failure to get up to speed on new threats," 29 percent named "lack of expertise with websites/applications," and 26 percent cited "IT staff failure to follow policies and procedures."[79]

However, targeted attacks by hackers are not uncommon and, when they do occur, the results can be disastrous, as the 2013 data breach at retail giant Target demonstrated. Further, examples of targeted attacks include the recent examples of ransomware attacks which targeted healthcare providers and other organizations. In recent cases, these ransomware attackers used hacking tools that exploited vulnerabilities in Microsoft software. The tools were stolen from the United States National Security Administration. Accordingly, an organization's ability to prevent data breaches should keep pace with the increasingly more sophisticated tools hackers employ to breach a system.

Finally, company insiders may intentionally mishandle information for their own gain or because they have a grudge against the company. A report issued by Verizon indicates that in 2016, 77% of data breaches involved an insider with a majority of these cases involving an individual carrying out data sabotage against their current or former employer as an act of retaliation.[80]

Although ideally your company's data protection systems are robust enough to ward off any data breach, sound business practice calls for having a system in place to respond to such incidents in order to minimize their effects. The following are steps that should be followed if you discover a data breach at your company, and should be taken into consideration in preparing a process for responding to data breaches:

1. *Notify Your Data Protection Officer ("DPO"):* Chapter One explained that a DPO is an individual who advises a company on relevant data protection law, develops company policies surrounding data protection, and ensures that the company complies with applicable laws. The complexity of the law and the potential magnitude for harm to your business should encourage most companies to appoint a DPO, either in-house or through a third-party provider that specializes in data protection services. Once a data breach is discovered, your DPO should be your first point of contact.

2. *Meet with Your Company's Data Incident Response Team:* Prior to experiencing a data breach, you should assemble a team of professionals who will oversee your company's response to future incidents. As such, it is important that a data incident response team is selected, but also that the members of the team understand their roles in the event of an incident and can quickly formulate a response. Ideally, your team will include people whose tasks include:

a. Taking corrective action to address the breach (IT, Operations)
b. Notifying the appropriate regulatory authorities (Legal)
c. Communicating the incident to employees (Communications, Human Relations)
d. Notifying customers and addressing subsequent customer and media inquiries (Public Relations, Human Relations, Customer Service)

Each of these steps is considered in greater detail below:

3. *Take Corrective Action to Address the Breach:* The "corrective action" that must be taken will depend on what caused the breach in the first place. Of course, further investigation may be needed to determine the cause. To the extent the origin of the breach is known, though, you should immediately act to protect further data loss. This may involve updating your company's security software, deactivating email or other accounts, changing passwords, or wiping data from devices.

4. *Notify the Appropriate Regulatory Authorities:* The appropriate authorities to contact in the event of a data breach depends on factors such as where your business is located, where your customers are located, and where your third-party vendors are located, if they were involved in the breach. It is possible (if not likely) that you will need to notify more than one legal authority. Therefore, it is critical that you and the legal representative on your Data Incident Response Team identify these legal authorities before a breach. By way of example, a company in the U.S. which is the subject of a breach involving health care information could be required to report the breach to credit bureaus, State Attorneys General, the Secretary of the U.S. Department of Health and Human Services, and even the media. If the data breach involved the theft or loss of hardware—such as laptops, personal tablets, or thumb drives—it may also be appropriate or necessary to notify local law enforcement.

5. *Notify Affected Parties:* After alerting legal authorities, your company's data breach response plan should address whether you will notify those whose data may have been compromised in the breach. The first question you might ask in this regard is whether you are legally required to notify your customers of a breach. Like notification of regulatory authorities, notification of customers depends on applicable law and should be determined with the help of your legal advisor. In the U.S., there is no federal law requiring customer notification, but there are notification laws in 48 states, the District of Columbia, the U.S. Virgin Islands, and Puerto Rico. Some states that require notification also specify the time frame in which individuals must be contacted and what information must be included in the notification. In jurisdictions outside the U.S. data the obligations incumbent on an organization can vary.

Country	Breach Notification Requirements
Argentina	There are no requirements to report data breaches to the NDPDP or to data subjects. However, all data incidents must be recorded by the data controller or processor. These records are subject to audit by the NDPDP.
Australia	There are no requirements to report data breaches to the OAIC.
Brazil	There are no requirements to report data breaches to regulatory authorities or subjects.
Canada	Only a handful of provincial privacy statutes require breach notification. However, the recently passed amendments (Digital Privacy Act) to PIPEDA would require notice of material breaches

	to be made to the OPC and to the individuals affected once these amendments take effect.
China	The Guideline recommends that Data Administrators should promptly notify a data breach to affected data subjects, and in case of major breach promptly report to the personal information protection management department. Under the Cybersecurity Law, network operators must promptly inform data subjects if their personal information is disclosed, tampered with or destroyed, and notification must also be made promptly to the relevant authorities.
EU	In the event of a data breach, the controller must report the breach to the DPA without undue delay, and in any event within 72 hours of becoming aware of it. There is an exception where the data breach is unlikely to result in any harm to data subjects.
Germany	The BDSG contains a breach notification duty which applies if: sensitive personal data, personal data subject to professional secrecy, personal data related to criminal and/or administrative offences, personal data concerning bank or credit card accounts, certain telecommunications and online data is abused or lost and an unauthorized third party acquires knowledge of said data. An organization should notify their relevant data protection authority and the data subjects effected.

India	In the event of a breach an organization should notify the Indian Computer Emergency Response Team (Cert-In) within a reasonable amount of time.
Japan	The APPI does not explicitly require notification to a ministry or governmental authority in the event of a leak or security breach that may lead to a leak of personal data, although a ministry may request that a report be submitted on a voluntary basis. The guidelines on this point are under preparation.
Netherlands	A data breach must be reported to the Autoriteit Persoonsgegevens and the data subject, if such data breach has or may have serious disadvantageous consequences for the protection of personal data.
Russia	There is no mandatory requirement to report data security breaches or losses to the Agency or to data subjects.
South Africa	A data breach must be reported to the Information Regulator and the data subject as soon as possible unless the identity of such data subject cannot be established.
United Kingdom	There is no mandatory requirement in the Act to report data security breaches or losses to the ICO unless "a large number of people are affected" or the consequences of the breach are particularly "serious", the ICO should be informed.
United States	Breach notification requirements vary by sector as there is not an overriding federal privacy law. 48 US states, Washington, D.C. and most US

	territories (including, Puerto Rico, Guam and the Virgin Islands) require notifying state residents of a security breach

In addition, if you have terms of service or a privacy policy for your business, you must notify customers in a manner consistent with that agreement. To read more about what should be included in your company's data privacy policy, see Chapter Seven.

Regardless of whether you are legally required to notify customers, it is probably a good idea to do so. After all, as data breach remediation service Intersections has said, "... customers have shown a propensity to stop doing business with companies that cannot protect their confidential information, and do not take care of their customers when a breach occurs."[81] For that reason, your incident response plan should include details such as how you will notify customers, what your notification will say, and when it will be issued. As such it is important to construct a security breach response plan that focuses on satisfying legal requirements if a security breach occurs and offers a systematic and timely way to notify customers of the breach, not only for compliance purposes but also as a matter of customer relations.

Finally, one important factor to note is that, if a law enforcement body is investigating the source or nature of a data breach at your company, you may be required to wait to notify customers. This ensures that sharing too much information will not compromise the investigation.

Address Customer Concerns and Deploy Public Relations: After taking care of legal requirements, your data breach incident plan should address your customers and clients. Specifically, this step of your plan should aim to make customers comfortable with continuing to do business with you.

> ### To Insource or Outsource
> ### Your Data Breach Incident Response Team
> You may not need to outsource every aspect of your data breach incident response team, but if your answer to any of the following is "no," you should strongly consider outsourcing the corresponding function of your incident response team:
>
> ✓ Do you have the IT capability to fix the problem that caused the breach?
>
> ✓ Do you have an in-house disaster recovery plan so you can continue to use your network securely after a breach?
>
> ✓ Do you have the personnel and systems in place to handle a significant increase in customer inquiries after a breach?

How do you do this? Primarily, by having a good customer support team in place to answer questions and address concerns. Additionally, some incident response plans offer affected individuals the option to enroll in free identity theft protection programs for a specified period of time. SMEs may find it beneficial to contract with a third party to provide these services if a data breach incident occurs.

This portion of your plan should also contemplate media relations: will you proactively reach out to media outlets about the breach through a press release, for example, or will you refer all media inquiries to a specified individual who has prepared discussion points? Addressing concerns arising from the public is also an important consideration in your plan. In the event negative information resulting from a data breach is posted online, one of the best policies is to remain proactive rather than react after the damage has been done. Issue a public statement and "stay ahead of the story." A public statement can come in the form of a press release or statement to a news source. Be certain to make clear and unambiguous statements regarding the issues that lead to the breach and emphasize that any lingering problems related to the issue are being remedied.

6. Test the Plan and Evaluate Your Response After an Incident: Once your plan is in place, you should test it for effectiveness. Often, you will discover gaps in your plan that were not initially apparent. If you contract with a third party to handle customer inquiries after a breach, for example, make sure they are familiar with your company's practices and that they know the size of the breach, so the call center is appropriately staffed. If your incident response team calls for the head of your IT department to handle the breach, appoint someone else to handle normal business-related technology matters in the meantime. Finally, although prospectively testing your plan will ensure a breach is handled as smoothly as possible, you should also evaluate your company's response after a data breach occurs. Doing so allows you to adjust your plan to address future breaches, should they arise, in an even more competent manner. Using a simulated breach will expose areas that are weak, providing time to make the necessary adjustments and engage your team in additional training.

Beyond Employee Training

Your vulnerability to data breaches depends largely on your employees. In addition to training, taking the following measures respecting employees will help minimize the chances of a data breach:

- ✓ Thoroughly investigate employees who will have access to personal data before hiring them, through background checks and verification of references;

- ✓ Have new employees sign an agreement stating they will abide by your company's data security practices and regularly remind employees of their duty to follow those practices;

- ✓ Limit employee access to personal data to those with a legitimate need to know;

- ✓ Create a system for ensuring that employees who leave the company or change positions no longer have access to personal data;

- ✓ Ensure that part-time, seasonal, and temporary workers also receive training;

- ✓ Require employees to notify the DPO as soon as they become aware of a potential data security breach, such as when a device is lost or stolen; and

- ✓ Institute penalties for violations of your data security protection policy.

B. Training

While a data breach incident response plan is aimed at helping your business respond to a breach after the fact, training is intended to minimize the risk of a breach occurring at all. Ideally, all of your company's employees should receive training in order to gain awareness of why it is important to secure personal information, learn how a data breach may occur, and understand how a breach may be prevented. As a rule, most jurisdictions do not have a rule that mandates data security training or provides guidance as to the content of this training, however the law in all jurisdictions requires organizations to take reasonable measures to safeguard data privacy. Therefore, training employees on data security would be viewed as a part of a larger obligation to maintain reasonable data security practices.

The first step in any training program should be raising awareness of the importance of securing personal information.

Real examples that relate to everyday workplaces help employees envisage security risks that they may not have considered before. Employees may not know, for example, the risk associated with emailing a document containing sensitive information to themselves. Before awareness training, they may consider this practice just a convenient way to work on a document at home. Once employees are attuned to the risks and potential for harm that can arise if they fail to follow data protection policies, they are more likely to observe best practices.

After raising awareness, data protection training should include the following elements:

- *Identifying Risks:* Identifying risks involves gaining familiarity with phishing, spyware, malware, computer viruses, and social engineering.[82]

• *Maintaining Physical Security:* Maintaining physical security extends from something as simple as locking windows and doors, to ensuring that computers are not left unlocked and unattended, to refraining from downloading documents on mobile devices.

• *Maintaining Cyber Security:* Maintaining cyber security covers items including password protecting documents, encrypting and securely transmitting files, and validating users of your company's network.

• *Following Technology Best Practices:* Technology "best practices" relate to ideal procedures for email and Internet usage, remote system and document access, and data backup.

• *Following Personal Information Protection Best Practices:* Personal information protection best practices involves knowing when and to what extent personal information may be used or disclosed, what notification must be given to individuals when collecting their personal information (such as the ability to opt out), and how to address individual requests for information. Best practices also involve knowing how long personal information may be retained and how to properly dispose of personal information.

• *Handling a Data Breach Incident:* Handling a data breach requires training as to what constitutes a data breach, who to notify in the event of a breach, and what your company's data breach incident response plan entails. Although it may seem counterintuitive to explain what constitutes a data breach, understanding the precise legal definition of when a data breach has occurred is important from a compliance perspective. Certainly, legislation can provide instruction on what constitutes a data breach, but any legislative definition can be expanded and additional duties arise pursuant to contracts between you company and customers, vendors and services providers. Many contracts include provisions that require notification in the event of a potential data breach. Understanding what constitutes a data breach not only assists an organization understand when it is required to notify customers that a data breach has occurred, but also provides guidance in preventing data breaches, as well.

C. Data Retention and Disposal

As discussed in Chapter Six, your data retention and disposal obligations are generally governed by the law in the jurisdiction (country, state, or territory, as the case may be) where you are located, where your customers are located, and where any third parties are located that you have contracted with to handle your customers' data.

As a general rule, it is a good idea to develop a data retention policy that complies with the most stringent of those laws. A data retention policy is a set of procedures that explains in what format and how long to keep a record before it should be destroyed. A retention policy may also specify how information may be securely disposed.

A solid data retention policy should consist of:

• *Policy Goals:* These may include retaining documents for future use, properly securing data that is stored, and correctly disposing of data in order to minimize the risk of future breach.

• *Document Retention Management:* Defining who is in charge of data retention and disposal practices and who can answer questions about the policy. Ideally, this would be the company's Data Protection Officer.

> ### The Data Retention Policy's Relationship to Your Privacy Policy
>
> If you think the advice to craft a data retention policy conforming to the most stringent of applicable laws sounds familiar, you are right. In Chapter Three, you were also advised to create a data privacy policy that complies with the strictest applicable laws. This repetition is intentional: not only is it good business practice, but also the data retention policy is often part of a company's overall data privacy policy. You will often find companies posting a privacy policy online that contains a data retention provision, and you may want to consider notifying customers of your data retention policy online as well.

• *Retention Requirements:* Retention requirements consist of types of records (email, tax records, bank records, etc.) and corresponding lengths of time that each type must be retained. Note that how long each type of document should be retained is not just a judgment call on the part of the organization. Instead, legal obligations often compel businesses to retain information for a certain period of time. How long data should be retained depends on the jurisdiction(s) in which an organization operates and the types of data the organization collects. For example, in the U.S., organizations engaged in financial transactions are subject to often stricter data retention requirements depending on the type of data being collected and the specific financial activity being conducted. Whereas, organizations that collect personal health information in electronic format are required by HIPAA to "section for 6 years from the date of its creation or the date when it last was in effect, whichever is later."[83]

Further, organizations may have a legal obligation to preserve data when a credible threat of litigation is presented. When an organization is presented with a "credible threat of litigation" is context-dependent. The duty to preserve data that may be relevant in potential litigation information is triggered when litigation is "reasonably anticipated."[84] The test for "reasonable anticipation of litigation" varies by jurisdiction, but, in general, reasonable anticipation of litigation arises when a party knows there is a credible threat that it will become involved in litigation.[85] The duty to preserve evidence does not imply that a party is not required to preserve "all its documents but rather only documents that the party knew or should have known were, or could be, relevant to the parties' dispute."[86] However, if an organization fails to retain records that may be requested in the discovery process by the other party, your company may face fines and penalties. As such, best practices dictate that an organization establish clear policies regarding data retention that consider retention obligations above the minimal legal requirements.

• *Storage Requirements:* Storage requirements will vary by document type and by format of the data (whether in tangible or electronic form). Companies often archive certain records in an off-site facility (if in tangible form) or using a third-party service (if in electronic form). Archiving data frees up valuable space, whether in the office or on the company network, by placing data in less accessible locations when only infrequent access is needed.

When considering how data is stored it is also important to consider legal requirements. For example, multiple countries including India, Switzerland, Germany, Australia and Canada have enacted laws restricting corporations from storing data outside their physical country borders. The recently enacted EU-U.S. Privacy Shield Framework mandates that companies operating within the European Union are forbidden from sending personally identifiable information (PII) outside the European economic area unless it is guaranteed that the data will receive equivalent levels of protection. Further, enterprises should ensure E.U. citizens' data will not make it into the hands of third parties outside the United States. These laws known as "data localization" can be defined as the act of storing data on a device that is physically located within the country where the data was created. Data localization requirements are governmental obligations that explicitly mandate local storage of personal information or strongly encourage local storage through data protection laws that erect stringent legal compliance obligations on cross-border data transfers.

• *Disposal Requirements:* Your data retention policy should also clarify how to responsibly dispose of data when no longer needed. Doing so will minimize the chances that sensitive and personal data will be mishandled in the future. For tangible documents, your policy should stress the importance of shredding sensitive and personal information. For electronic data, know that deleting information from a computer hard drive is not enough to destroy the data. Instead, your policy should require those in charge of data disposal to use a process called "degaussing" (destroying the magnetic alignment of the hard drive or backup tape) or to hire a reputable third party to destroy the data. Data wiping software that overwrites data may also be an option, but be aware that the U.S. Department of Defense advises companies to overwrite the data at least seven times before the hard drive is then discarded.

Organizations who handle personal information or other sensitive data may be required under the laws of the jurisdiction in which data is collected, processed or stored to follow specific guidelines when disposing of these data. These guidelines vary by jurisdiction, whether the organization operates in the public or private sector, and the type of data being collected.

Properly Disposing of Personal Data

In addition to the data disposal techniques outlined in this chapter, the following will help you ensure personal data is securely discarded at your company:

- ✓ Make shredders or locked shred bins (whereby documents cannot be retrieved once thrown away) easily accessible throughout your building.

- ✓ Make employees aware that throwing computer documents away by clicking "delete" or moving them to the trashcan folder does not delete the file from the computer's hard drive.

- ✓ Ensure that employees who work remotely abide by your document retention and disposal policy, including procedures for shredding documents containing personal data and discarding old computers and devices.

Note that if you are a U.S. company that uses consumer credit reports in your business, you may have to abide by the FTC's Disposal Rule which states, "Any person who maintains or otherwise possesses consumer information for a business purpose must properly dispose of such information by taking reasonable measures to protect against unauthorized access to or use of the information in connection with its disposal." 16 CFR 682.3

D. Enforcement Actions

Companies that experience a data breach incident will frequently find themselves the defendant in a lawsuit brought by individuals whose data was compromised in the breach or by regulatory authorities in charge of overseeing compliance with data protection laws.

In order to better understand and defend against these lawsuits, it is helpful to know what types of suits may be brought. Private individuals or a class of private individuals may bring a tort lawsuit alleging an organization was negligent in protecting data it collected or breach of contract, or statutory private rights of action under federal or state law or that a company misrepresented its cybersecurity policy. Further, regulators may bring suit or impose fines that are specified in the applicable data protection laws. In cases involving serious violations the penalties can be significant. For example, the GDPR authorizes allows DPAs to issue fines for serious infringements up to a maximum of the greater of €20 million or four percent of worldwide turnover.[87]

Often, one data breach incident will result in both private and regulator lawsuits.

Tort Lawsuits

Under U.S. state tort laws, individuals may sue companies for data breaches resulting in harm to individuals. After retail giant Target was hacked in late 2013, leading to the theft of data on approximately 40 million credit and debit cards, several class action lawsuits were filed by individuals whose data were compromised in the breach. One of those, filed in a federal District Court in Minnesota, claimed Target was negligent in securing its customers' personal data, and that its negligence led to the data breach.

Internet titan Google was also the subject of a number of class action lawsuits based on tort claims in 2013, after individuals alleged the company collected personal information, including emails and passwords, from unencrypted Wi-Fi networks. The private class action suits accompanied global regulatory action against Google for the same practice of collecting personal information, as discussed further below.

Tort actions to remedy data breaches have also been used in Canadian courts. Various Canadian common law courts have recognized the tort the doctrine of 'intrusion upon seclusion' as a legal theory of recovery for victims of data breaches[88]. Under this theory of recovery Canadian courts recognize that in the context of data breach cases, the tort of intrusion upon seclusion requires intentional and reckless conduct, without legal justification, giving rise to a 'highly offensive' intrusion into a person's privacy. Under this cause of action a claimant is not required to establish actual proof of economic loss which, provides a significant opportunity for the claimant who may have had their privacy breached, yet have been fortunate to not suffer actual economic losses such as often occurs in the wake of identity theft to press a claim against defendant organizations. Further this liberal standard has resulted in an uptick in class action claims arising from data breaches.

Breach of Contract Lawsuits

Another ground for a private lawsuit relating to a data breach is breach of the company's privacy statement. Although the point is arguable, many courts agree that a privacy statement creates a binding agreement between the company and the customer. When a company experiences a data breach or discloses personal information, customers may say that the company breached its agreement by failing to follow the privacy statement. The difficulty in this argument in proving damages—that the customers suffered harm as a result of the company's breach. In a recent groundbreaking case, the U.S. Court of Appeals for the Eleventh Circuit allowed class-action claims pertaining to negligence and breach of contract, to remain and remanded the case back to the district court. The parties reached a settlement believed to be the first in which victims of the data breach were compensated without having to show they suffered damages from a data breach.

This sort of lawsuit arose in 2010, when a class of individuals filed suit in the District of California claiming that Apple shared their iPhone and iPad unique identifiers to Apple app developers, which allowed the developer to track their devices. This lawsuit was one of four based on similar claims. Later that year, the judge in the District of California case dismissed the case on the grounds that none of the consumers could show that they had read the privacy agreement and therefore, none could prove he or she relied on the agreement.

Regulatory Actions

In addition to private lawsuits, regulators are bringing suits against companies for breach of data privacy agreements. The relevant data protection law determines maximum penalties and fines in these suits and, although they often seem minuscule when assessed against a large, international corporation, they might be devastating to a small- or mid-sized company.

In May 2017, the French privacy regulator fined Facebook €145,000 (about USD165,000) Facebook for inappropriately collecting and using consumer data. The action by the French privacy regulator coincided with similar regulatory actions by the Dutch and Belgian privacy regulators.[89] This alleged practice also led to several consumer class-action lawsuits against Facebook spearheaded by privacy advocates who allege the company intentionally flouts EU data privacy protections.[90]

Another notable enforcement action against a large company for violation of privacy laws began in July 2013, when the U.S. Federal Trade Commission ("FTC") filed a complaint against Samsung. In its suit, the FTC alleging that famous rapper Jay-Z's smartphone app, released in collaboration with Samsung, violated privacy laws by accessing significantly more information on users' phones than was necessary to enable the app.

Under U.S. law, the FTC can file suit on behalf of consumers for violations of consumers' privacy under section 5 of the Federal Trade Commission (FTC) Act which gives the FTC broad authority to investigate "unfair and deceptive acts and practices in or affecting commerce". The FTC has recently been active in enforcement actions involving website operators who fail to adhere to their stated data privacy policies and practices.

To avoid enforcement actions and civil claims, plan in advance. Develop and implement a sound data privacy policy, develop safeguards to prevent unintended access or disclosure of personal or sensitive information. Train internal staff and repeat training on a regular schedule, update the data privacy policy as need and implement reasonable data retention and disposal policies.

References

[79] Adam Greenberg, (2017). Human error cited as leading contributor to breaches, study shows. online SC Media US. Available at: https://www.scmagazine.com/study-find-carelessness-among-top-human-errors-affecting-security/article/535928/ Accessed 1 Jul. 2017.

[80] Ogden, J. (2017). 8 Examples of Internal-Caused Data Breaches. online Cimcor.com. Available at: https://www.cimcor.com/blog/8-examples-of-insider-internal-caused-data-breaches Accessed 1 Jul. 2017.

[81] DATA BREACH READINESS, INTERSECTIONS 1 (2011), *available at* http://www.intersections.com/library/7%20Steps%20to%20Breach%20Readiness%20WEB%20042810.pdf.

[82] "Social engineering" is non-technical criminal activity carried out with the assistance of unsuspecting persons. For example, a very official sounding caller requests access to business computers to "fix" a computer bug or any other contrived reason.

[83] 45 C.F.R. § 164.316(b)(2)

[84] *Rimkus Consulting Group, Inc. v. Cammarata*, 688 F. Supp. 2d 598, 612-613 n. 7 (S.D. Tex. 2010).

[85] *Zubulake v. UBS Warburg* LLC, 220 F.R.D. 212, 217 (S.D.N.Y. 2003).

[86] *Blue Sky Travel et al. v. Al Tayyer Group*, No. 13-2500 (4th Cir. Mar. 31, 2015),

[87] Art.83(5)-(6)

[88] *Jones v. Tsige*, 2012 ONCA 32

[89] Ft.com. (2017). Facebook faces more hurdles after Europe fine. online Available at: https://www.ft.com/content/0cfb056c-3bd0-11e7-821a-6027b8a20f23?mhq5j=e1 Accessed 12 Jul. 2017.

[90] Griffin, A. (2017). Why you could be owed £362 by Facebook. online The Independent. Available at: http://www.independent.co.uk/life-style/gadgets-and-tech/news/facebook-users-sue-site-over-data-collection-demand-compensation-for-privacy-breaches-10164481.html Accessed 12 Jul. 2017

CHAPTER SEVEN - THE DATA PRIVACY POLICY

A. Introduction

All businesses must comply with the data protection laws of the countries in which their customers live. These internal compliance rules must be in place before providing services or products to international as well as local customers. Drafting a strong data privacy policy that takes into account relevant legal obligations and ensuring that businesses and third-party vendors adhere to its terms are challenging tasks. Further the laws of certain jurisdictions require organizations with an online presence maintain a privacy policy that can accessed by their users. Additionally, some jurisdictions specify what terms must be contained in a privacy policy. Not only is it necessary to draft a privacy policy it is also important to consider drafting the data privacy policy to comport with the strictest data protection law that will be applicable to your business. Knowing which laws apply to your business and its customers is discussed in detail in Chapter Four, under "Multijurisdictional Conflicts in Data Privacy Laws."

B. What Should Be Included in a Data Privacy Policy?

The exact contents of an organization's privacy policy will depend upon the applicable law and may need to address requirements across geographical boundaries and legal jurisdictions. Broadly speaking, the data privacy policy should contain the following basic elements:

a) Notification to the data subject that personal information is being collected;

b) The company's policy regarding notification of changes in the data privacy policy;

c) The company's policy regarding notification in the event of a breach;

d) How personal information will be stored;

e) Whether and under what circumstances personal information will be shared with others (including parties related and unrelated to your business); and

f) Consent from the data subject.

Items d) through f) above should be further subdivided and treated differently based on the type of data involved: personal data, sensitive personal data, and publicly available information. For instance, your data privacy policy may not guarantee customers the same level of security in storage for personal information as it does for sensitive personal information. Each category of data is discussed below.

C. Data Classification

The information that a company collects from users generally falls within the following three categories:

1. Personal Data

The definition of personal data varies among data protection laws.

U.S. privacy laws commonly refer to personal data as "personally identifiable information," or "PII". Most federal agencies and data privacy laws define PII as information that "… can be used to distinguish or trace an individual's identity, such as their name, social security number, biometric records, etc. alone, or when combined with other personal or identifying information which is linked or linkable to a specific individual, such as date and place of birth, mother's maiden name, etc."[91]

The GDPR, in contrast, defines protected identifiable information or as it is known under the GDPR "personal data" in a more generalized manner. The law defines as "personal data" as "any information relating to an identified or identifiable natural person ("data subject"); an identifiable person is one who can be identified, directly or indirectly, in particular by reference to an identifier such as a name, an identification number, location data, online identifier or to one or more factors specific to the physical, physiological, genetic, mental, economic, cultural or social identity of that person."[92]

> ## How Your Company Should Classify its Data: The Privacy Audit
>
> To sort your personal data and sensitive personal data from other data your company collects, you should conduct a **data privacy audit.** If your company does not already have an individual or team in place that is knowledgeable in information technology audits, you may want to hire an outside firm to perform an audit. Even if you do not retain an outside firm, you can still build a data map to track the flow of information in your company to make sure your company is in compliance with applicable laws and to draft a better privacy policy. Some questions to ask in creating your data map include:
>
> - ✓ What types of data are you collecting (personal data, sensitive personal data, or publicly available information)?
> - ✓ Why are you collecting the data?
> - ✓ How is the data collected?
> - ✓ Where is the data stored?
> - ✓ Who has authority to access the data and who else may be able to access it?
> - ✓ Is the data being transferred anywhere?
> - ✓ What security systems are in place to protect the data?
> - ✓ What systems are in place to alert you if the data is lost or misused?
> - ✓ What systems are in place for destroying the data?

Sensitive Personal Data

Sensitive personal data is any information about an individual's:

- • Physical or mental health condition
- • Sex life

• Membership in trade unions

• Commission of any offence or criminal record

• Racial or ethnic origin

• Political opinions

• Financial information, or

• Children's personal information

Currently, the EU Data Protection Directive forbids processing information revealing sensitive personal data except where the data subject gives his or her explicit consent, or where one of a limited number of exceptions applies. The GDPR also contains similar restrictions and offers an expanded definition of sensitive personal information defined as, "Sensitive Personal Data" are personal data, revealing racial or ethnic origin, political opinions, religious or philosophical beliefs, trade-union membership; data concerning health or sex life and sexual orientation; genetic data or biometric data."[93]

The U.S. Department of Homeland Security defines sensitive personal data (which it refers to as "Sensitive Personally Identifiable Information") as "Personally Identifiable Information, which if lost, compromised, or disclosed without authorization, could result in substantial harm, embarrassment, inconvenience, or unfairness to an individual."[94] Sensitive Personally Identifiable Information can include, is not limited to: social security numbers; bank account number; healthcare related information; insurance information; academic records; credit and debit card numbers and driver's license and state ID information. Any such data collected must be handled more carefully than personal data because of the heightened risks in the event of a data breach.

2. *Publicly Available Information*

Publicly available data refers to published information that can be used, analyzed or obtained without requesting permission from the data subject. Some common examples include criminal justice data, public opinion polls, research journals, and business reports. Publicly available data does not include any personal identifiers that can be used to identify specific individuals such as names, photos, medical records or dates of birth.

Data that is in the public domain or are either fully anonymized (i.e. data from which no individuals can be identified) are generally outside the scope of data privacy laws.

Combining Personal Information from Multiple Sources

Collected personal information can, in some instances, be combined with information from other sources. Once combined, it may become easier to identify specific individuals. For example, a company may choose to combine a customer's geographical location with his personal information. The combined information will be treated as personal information as long as it is combined.[95]

D. Collecting and Processing Personal Information

The role your business plays in the processing of personal information determines its legal obligations, and understanding this role will result in a more suitable data privacy policy. Therefore, it is helpful to examine the various roles involved in the collection and processing of personal information.

Buying and Selling Customer Information Databases

If you buy or sell databases containing customer personal information, then you are a data controller and are obligated to secure that information.

Databases of customers' personal information may be bought or sold in limited circumstances where a business is insolvent, bankrupt, being shut down, or being sold. The buyer must only use the information for the purpose for which it was originally collected. Additionally, the buyer should notify customers of the change in ownership and must obtain consent if it wants to use information for a different purpose.

Data Controller

The Data Controller ("DC") is the person or legal entity responsible for determining the manner in which any type of personal information is to be processed and the purpose for processing the information. The DC decides what personal information will be collected, how it will be processed, under what conditions it will be disclosed to others and how it will be stored.

What is the difference between a DC and a DPO? A DC is an individual or legal entity responsible for the storage and utilization of personal information in either a computer or structured manual file. DCs can be legal entities such as companies, voluntary organizations and governmental branches. Your business is a DC if it controls and is responsible for the personal data it collects and holds. Under the GDPR a data controller is defined as "Controller" the natural or legal person, public authority, agency or any other body which alone or jointly with others determines the purposes and means of the processing of personal data; where the purposes and means of processing are determined by EU or Member State laws, the controller (or the criteria for nominating the controller) may be designated by those laws.[96]

A DPO, on the other hand, is an individual assigned to ensure that data privacy policies are in place, comply with the relevant laws and is available to data subjects for rectification and deletion of personal information.

Data Processor

A Data Processor, acts in compliance with the instructions of the DC and can be any person, other than an employee of the DC, who is responsible for processing data on behalf of the DC. The GDRP provides a general definition of data processing. The law defines data processing, as any operation or set of operations performed upon personal data or sets of personal data, whether or not by automated means, such as collection, recording, organization, structuring, storage, adaptation or alteration, retrieval, consultation, use, disclosure by transmission, dissemination or otherwise making available, alignment or combination, restriction, erasure or destruction.[97]

A data processor will normally be a third-party vendor providing services to your business, that assists in the collection, storage and use of the personal data collected.

Determining Whether Outside Vendors are Data Controllers or Data Processors

Your DPO should determine which outside vendors are considered data controllers and which are data processors. Data privacy laws generally treat these two categories differently. Data processors are not directly subject to the EU Data Directive. Instead, data collectors who use third-party data processors are responsible for ensuring the third party's compliance with the law.

When using a data processor –

- ✓ ensure adequate security measures are in place
- ✓ require return, destruction or deletion of personal data that is no longer needed
- ✓ prohibit disclosure to third parties
- ✓ include a right to audit the data processor's compliance
- ✓ include an indemnity or damages provision for breaches of your contract.

E. Required Provisions

The following are standard provisions that should be included in your data privacy policy; these do not change depending on the category of information being collected, used, or disclosed.

Notice and Consent

Notice

The data privacy policy itself is a form of notice given to the customer, often as part of the terms and conditions of a company's website. In many cases, the terms and conditions of use for a website become part of the data privacy policy by reference. The "Notice" provision tells your customers what information you collect and what you do with the information. The customer can use this to choose whether or not to participate by providing consent. Data privacy laws, as a general matter, express a preference toward clear and easily recognized data privacy policies that a user can easily find and understand. A 2013 report presented before Canada's Standing Committee on Access to Information, Privacy and Ethics summarizes a benchmark standard that data privacy policies should adhere regarding the notice they provide users. The report points to the fact that proper notice of data use practices is achieved through transparency. To this effect the report states, "Privacy policies should have a full description of what information is collected, for what purposes it is used, and with whom it is shared. Privacy policies should be easily accessible, simple to read, and accurate.

Organizations should regularly review their privacy policies and update them as necessary."[98]

Consent
✓ Must be obtained from the person whose personal information is being collected
✓ Easy to understand
✓ Clear and straightforward
✓ Clearly explain how the personal information will be used
✓ In the case of children, consent must be obtained by parent or legal guardian
✓ May need to be renewed when the data privacy policy or the use to be made changes from that originally stated.

Consent

The data privacy policy must contain a consent provision by which a data subject agrees, either implicitly or expressly, to the processing of personal information. Implied consent means that, by virtue of using a company's website, a data subject is deemed to agree with the terms of the site, including the data privacy policy. Most data privacy laws allow consent to be implied if notice of the privacy policy is clearly given on the website and if the data subject has the option to opt out of the terms somewhere on the website. Express consent, on the other hand, means that the data subject explicitly agrees to the terms of the data privacy policy. This is usually achieved by requiring customers to click "I agree" at the bottom of the privacy policy. This method of obtaining consent is an example of an "opt-in" framework.

What constitutes proper consent varies by jurisdiction. However, at its foundation some common characteristics can be identified regarding valid consent as to consent to data collection practices. The GDPR states "Consent" means any freely given, specific, informed and unambiguous indication of the data subject's agreement to the processing of his or her personal data. Consent must be given by a statement or a clear affirmative action.[99] Consent must reflect the data subject's genuine and free choice. If there is any element of compulsion, or undue pressure put upon the data subject, consent will not be valid. Blanket consent that does not specify the exact purpose of the processing is not valid consent. In order for consent to be valid, data subjects must be provided with sufficient information to enable them to understand what they are consenting to. Where any processing activity is performed on the basis of consent, the controller must be able to demonstrate that it has obtained valid consent from the affected data subjects.

Protection

Once personal data is collected, it must be kept safe and secure from potential abuse, loss or theft. The measures taken to protect personal information must be commercially reasonable; otherwise, the data controller and data processor will be liable for breaches. Your privacy policy should include a description of processes used to secure personal information, which may include the use of Secure Socket Layer ("SSL") technology to encrypt personal information sent over the Internet, your commitment to training employees to handle personal data appropriately, and practices such as security audits or review of third-party vendor agreements for compliance with your privacy policy. As a general rule data controllers are responsible for ensuring that personal data are kept secure, by a variety of internal and external means.[100]

Access

Data subjects must be given access to their personal data and the ability to correct any inaccuracies. Although not yet globally mandated, this should be the standard going forward as the trend in newer legislation is to require this ability to access. Your privacy policy should notify customers of the manner in which they may request access to their personal data. Data privacy law in a number of jurisdictions requires data controllers to provide data subjects with access to their personal data. The procedures for allowing access to data and the recourse for correcting inaccurate information varies by jurisdiction.

Rectification, Erasure, and Blocking of Data

The privacy policy must recognize the data subject's right to rectification of inaccurate data and the right to the erasure or blocking of data whenever the processing of such data does not comply with applicable laws, regulations and consent of the data subject.

Notice of Changes and Notice of Breach

The privacy policy must explain the process for notification of changes in the privacy policy and data breaches. Possible notification options include periodic emails, or requesting the customer to visit the website frequently to be informed of any notice of change. Where the website requires a user to log in with a secure password, the notice of change and an accompanying request to renew their approval can be shown upon login. As a general matter data privacy policies should err on the side of clarity and transparency. As such, notice of changes in policy and notices of breaches of information should be made as soon as possible. Given that the requirements in this area a data controller must follow can vary by jurisdiction it is important to consult with the relevant laws of the jurisdiction in which data collection, processing and storage takes place.

Make Sure Your Company's Privacy Policy is Effective

✓ **Make it visible.** You should link to a detailed privacy policy from your home page, and make sure the link itself is easy to see when visitors first enter your site. A prominent link to the policy should also be displayed on each page where you collect information from the customer.

✓ **Make it easy to read.** Customers do not want to read technical or legal jargon in your policy. They should easily be able to understand what you are doing with their information.

✓ **Make sure you do what you say you will.** If you say you provide employee training on data security twice annually, confirm that you have a system in place to actually do so. Otherwise, employees who communicate with customers could unwittingly divulge the lack of adherence in casual conversations, leading to customer mistrust. Your lack of adherence could also be the basis for a lawsuit.

✓ **Make sure you review it regularly.** Your business practices will naturally change over time, so review your policy at recurring intervals to verify that your practices and policy align.

References

[91] OFFICE OF MGMT. & BUDGET, EXEC. OFFICE OF THE PRESIDENT, OMB MEMO NO. M-07-16, SAFEGUARDING AGAINST AND RESPONDING TO THE BREACH OF PERSONALLY IDENTIFIABLE INFORMATION 1 n.1 (2007), *available at* http://www.whitehouse.gov/omb/memoranda/fy2007/m07-16.pdf

[92] Art.4(1)

[93] Art.9(1)

[94] U.S. DEPT. OF HOMELAND SECURITY, HANDBOOK FOR SAFEGUARDING SENSITIVE PERSONALLY IDENTIFIABLE INFORMATION (2015), *available at*

https://www.dhs.gov/sites/default/files/publications/Handbook%20for%20Safeg
uarding%20Sensitive%20PII_0.pdf

[95] OFFICE OF MGMT. & BUDGET, EXEC. OFFICE OF THE PRESIDENT, OMB MEMO
NO. M-10-23, GUIDANCE FOR AGENCY USE OF THIRD-PARTY WEBSITES AND
APPLICATIONS 8 (2010), *available at*
http://www.whitehouse.gov/sites/default/files/omb/assets/memoranda_2010/m1
0-23.pdf (Updating the Office of Management and Budget's official definition
of personally identifiable information (PII) to clarify that "non-PII can become
PII whenever additional information is made publicly available . . . that, when
combined with other available information, could be used to identify an
individual").

[96] Art.4(7)

[97] Art.4(2)

[98] Priv.gc.ca. (2017). Guidelines for Online Consent - Office of the Privacy
Commissioner of Canada. online Available at: https://www.priv.gc.ca/en/privacy-
topics/collecting-personal-information/consent/gl_oc_201405/   Accessed 6 Jul.
2017.

[99] Art.4(11), 6(1)(a), 7

[100] See Art.5(1)(f), 24(1), 25(1)-(2), 28, 39, 32[1] See Art.5(1)(f), 24(1), 25(1)-(2),
28, 39, 32.

SAMPLE PRIVACY POLICY TEMPLATE

A data privacy policy should be easy to find and, at a minimum, clearly describe what data is being collected, its intended use, and the company's data retention policies. The following is a template with suggested principal sections and coverage.

What personal information you supply to us and how we use it. Describe the personal information that will be collected directly from the customer. For example: *We will ask for your name, email address, phone number and, if you are purchasing our products or services, a credit card number, shipping address. To better serve you, you may supply us with your age, gender, and other personal information. We use this information to fulfill your purchase orders, improve your future shopping experiences or communicate with you.*

What personal information is being collected automatically, including from mobile devices and how we use it. Describe any personal information that will be collected automatically (e.g. from the use of cookies), even if the information is anonymous or can be anonymized. For Example: *Our website uses cookies and may collect information about your browsing history or preferences. If you access our website from a mobile device we may receive and collect your mobile device number. We use this information to provide you with a more personalized shopping experience.*

Giving your consent to collect personal information. Describe the options customers have to provide or withhold consent to the collection of personal information and/or the use of cookies. Always outline a choice, whether it is an opt-in choice, as required by the more stringent data privacy laws (like the EU Directives and the upcoming GDPR) or an opt-out choice as is acceptable in the U.S. For example: *You may choose not to provide personal information. If required for making a purchase, we may not be able to complete your purchase. You may decide not to allow cookies to be used, however, some services on our website may not be available. You must indicate your choice by clicking the opt-out option.* (If you choose to use an opt-in or express consent option, indicate this by requiring the opt-in choice be made before continuing to the website).

Sharing of personal information with others. Describe under what circumstances personal information may be shared, and the types of companies that might receive your customer's personal information. For example: *In order to provide a better experience and service, we may provide your personal information to our related companies or affiliates, third party service providers, and other businesses for marketing purposes. When we share personal information, we do not provide credit card or other financial information.*

How secure is my personal information. Describe the security measures your company has in place. This description may be general or specific, such as describing encryption or any other specific technology tools employed in securing personal information. For example: *Security of your personal information is important to us. We have appropriate security measures in place to protect against loss, misuse or alteration of information collected from you. We use software that encrypts information you provide to us.*

EU-U.S. and Swiss-U.S. Privacy Shield Frameworks. If your business is located in the U.S. and you expect to deal with customers located in the EU, include information about whether your business participates in the EU-U.S. and Swiss-U.S. Privacy Shield Frameworks, together with a link to the U.S. Department of Commerce website which contains a list of all self-certified U.S. companies participating in these programs.

Access and contact information. Provide information on how customers can access their personal information to make corrections or changes. Provide a contact individual (job title is sufficient) together with contact details.

Additional provisions. There may be specific regulatory requirements that must be included, based on the location of expected website visitors.

This template is available online at:

www.intersticeconsulting.com/ibtt/tradeandtaxation/data-privacy/policy-template

HOW TO KEEP UPDATED

We offer a variety of ways for readers to stay updated on the latest developments in data privacy laws:

1. Subscription service:

The first thing you should do is register online with proof of purchase (such as the receipt number from your online purchase) at www.intersticeconsulting.com/ibtt/tradeandtaxation/data-privacy/updates and you'll automatically receive six months of updates to the materials covered in this book. Beyond six months, we will offer a paid subscription service.

2. Online training:

We are currently developing a web-based training course which will review aspects of the materials covered in this book. The course's release date has not been finalized but is foreseen to occur before the end of 2017.

3. Corporate training courses:

Our professionals are available to lead corporate training courses for companies of all sizes. The typical training would occur over a half day (3-5 hours).

4. Individual consultations:

Specific cases can be discussed via telephone or email, at our prevailing hourly consulting rates.

5. Outsourced DPO services:

OVERVIEW OF ACTIVITIES: An Outsourced Data Privacy and Security Officer (ODPO) can fulfill a number of functions designed to meet an organization's current and future data privacy and security needs. Generally, the ODPO oversees all activities an in-house Data Privacy Officer would perform, provided by a data privacy and security expert rather than simply assigning the same tasks to an administrator or manager.

Services offered:

• Identify, implement, and maintain organization's data privacy policies and procedures in coordination with organization management, administration, and legal counsel.

• Information privacy risk and compliance audits.

• Ensure the organization has and maintains appropriate privacy consent, authorization, and information notices and materials reflecting current organization policies, in compliance with the relevant laws.

• Organize, direct, deliver, or ensure delivery of privacy training and awareness to all employees, contractors, alliances, and other appropriate third parties.

• Develop, implement, and monitor ongoing compliance of all trading partners and vendors to ensure all privacy concerns, requirements, and responsibilities are addressed.

• Establish a process to track access to protected information, as required by law, compiling quarterly reports from collected statistics.

• Implement a process for receiving, documenting, tracking, investigating, and taking action on all complaints concerning the organization's privacy policies.

• Provide continuous access to specialized and up-to-date legal knowledge.

• Develop procedures to be triggered upon the unauthorized release of protected information, ensuring full compliance with relevant data privacy and security laws.

Data Privacy Audits

There are typically three stages to auditing your data protection standards:

(1) Initial meeting with management to review data protection policies and procedures and to agree timing and arrangements for the audit itself.

(2) On site audit, comprising principally of interviews with staff from the various business departments, but also including an inspection tour of your premises, directly observing data handling practice.

(3) An off-site review by us of your existing data protection related documentation, e.g.

• Data protection policies
• Codes of practice
• Privacy statements
• Information security policies
• Access controls
• Incident logs
• Subject access request logs
• Report logs (whether to the DPC or direct to data subjects)
• Training material
• Employment contracts
• Contracts with clients
• Contracts with service providers

The deliverable from our audit is a report on your current state of compliance and recommended measures to address any shortfalls.

For all enquiries, please send an email to: dataprivacy@intersticeconsulting.com

APPENDIX

Multijurisdictional Data Privacy Matrix

Country	Argentina	Australia
Regulatory and Enforcement Agency/Privacy Laws	National Directorate for Personal Data Protection (NDPDP) Personal Data Protection Law Number 25,326 (PDPL), generally regulates the collection and use of personal data and sensitive information.	Australian Information Commissioner ("OAIC") The Federal Privacy Act 1988 (Privacy Act) and the Australian Privacy Principles (APPs) provide a regulatory framework for the handling of personal information or sensitive information by an entity that carries on business in Australia or collects personal data in Australia.
Protected Personal Information Defined	The PDPL defines personal information or personal data as any type of information related to identified or identifiable individuals or legal entities. Protected personal information can be collected provided the subject provides proper consent to collection.	The Privacy Act defines protected personal information as Information or an opinion about an identified individual, or an individual who is reasonably identifiable, whether the information or opinion is true or not, and whether the information or opinion is recorded in material form or not.
Sensitive Information Defined	Personal information revealing racial or ethnic origin, political views, religious beliefs, philosophical or moral stands, union affiliations or any information referring to health or sexual life. Sensitive information cannot be collected or used for commercial purposes.	The Privacy Act defines sensitive information or an opinion about: • racial or ethnic origin • political opinions • membership of a political association • religious beliefs or affiliations • philosophical beliefs • membership of a professional or trade association • membership of a trade union

		• sexual orientation or practices • criminal record that is also personal information • health information about an individual • genetic information about an individual that is not otherwise health information • biometric information that is to be used for the purpose of automated biometric identification or verification, or • biometric templates.
Breach Notification Requirements	There are no requirements to report data breaches to the NDPDP or to data subjects. However, all data incidents must be recorded by the data controller or processor. These records are subject to audit by the NDPDP.	There are no requirements to report data breaches to the OAIC.
Data Disposal Requirements	Under the PDPL, once personal data is no longer needed for the purpose for which it was required, it must be destroyed.	The Privacy Act states an organization can only retain for as long as it is needed for the purposes it was collected. Once the data is no longer needed an organization must take reasonable steps to destroy or permanently de-identify (anonymize) personal information.
Data Controller and Processor Registration Requirements	Under the PDPL requires controllers and processors register with the NDPDP.	The Privacy Act does not require controllers and processors to register with OAIC.
Data Protection Officer Requirements	None	None
Access, Rectification, and Deletion Requirements	Under the PDPL individuals and corporations have the right to access their personal data held by a data controller and may request deletion of their data only if the personal data is inaccurate.	An organization must, on request by an individual, give that individual access to the personal information (and the ability to correct inaccurate information.

Consent and Notice Requirements	The PDPL requires that the prior to collection of information from a subject, the individual must provide their consent given freely and expressly. The subject must also be notified of the conditions under which the personal data will be used.	Prior to collection of information from a subject, the individual must provide their consent given freely and expressly. The subject must also be notified of the conditions under which the personal data will be used.

Country	**Brazil**	**Canada**
Regulatory and Enforcement Agency/Privacy Laws	CGI.br, ANATEL, the National Consumer Secretariat and the Brazilian System to Defend Competition Federal Law No. 12.965/2014 ("Brazilian Internet Act") and Decree No. 8.771/16 ("Decree"), provides limited regulation on security and processing of personal data.	Office of the Privacy Commissioner of Canada ('OPC') Personal Information Protection and Electronic Documents Act ('PIPEDA') In addition to the three-chief federal Acts governing use of personal information, each Canadian province and territory has enacted data privacy laws that govern the collection and processing of personal information.
Protected Personal Information Defined	The Decree defines personal data as any "data related to identified or identifiable natural person, including identifying numbers, electronic identifiers or locational data, when these are related to a person".	PIPEDA defines personal information as any information about an identifiable individual.
Sensitive Information Defined	Not defined under current Brazilian law.	Not defined under current Canadian law.
Breach Notification Requirements	There are no requirements to report data breaches to regulatory authorities or subjects.	Only a handful of provincial privacy statutes require breach notification. However, the recently passed amendments (Digital Privacy Act) to PIPEDA would require notice of material breaches to be made to the OPC and to the individuals affected once these amendments take effect.
Data Disposal Requirements	None	Personal information can be retained only as long as necessary for the disclosed purposes.
Data Controller and Processor	Brazilian law does not require controllers and processors to register with CGI.br, ANATEL, the	Canadian law does not require controllers and processors to

Registration Requirements	National Consumer Secretariat and the Brazilian System to Defend Competition	register with OPC or provincial authorities.
Data Protection Officer Requirements	None	PIPEDA, PIPA Alberta, PIPA BC and PIPITPA expressly require organizations to appoint a data processing officer.
Access, Rectification, and Deletion Requirements	Consumers are entitled to have access to personal data and databases about themselves and to demand immediate correction whenever they find that the data or files are incorrect.	All Canadian privacy statutes require a data collector or processor allow a subject a right of access to personal information held by an organization and a right to correct inaccuracies in/update their personal information records.
Consent and Notice Requirements	The Decree requires free, informed and express consent of Internet user is required for the collection, use, storage, transfer and treatment of personal data on-line.	All Canadian privacy statutes requires free, informed and express consent of a data subject for the collection, use, storage, transfer and treatment of personal data online.

Country	**China**	**EU**
Regulatory and Enforcement Agency/Privacy Laws	No centralized enforcement agency. The Decision on Strengthening Online Information Protection National Standard of Information Security Technology – Guideline for Personal Information Protection within Information System for Public and Commercial Services GB/Z 28828-2012; the 'Guideline')	Each Member State will be required to appoint one or more agencies responsible for enforcement and regulation.
Protected Personal Information Defined	Any electronic information which can enable identification of a citizen's individual identity. This can include consumer personal information as a consumer's name, gender, occupation, date of birth, identification document number, residential address, contact information, status of income and assets, health status, consumption habits, identifying biological characteristics and other information collected by business operators during their provision of goods or services that may, independently or	Any information relating to an identified or identifiable natural person.

	in combination with other information, identify the consumer.	
Sensitive Information Defined	The Guideline defines sensitive personal as personal information the leakage or alteration of which may result in adverse impact to the data subject. This can include personal identification number, mobile phone number, race, political view, religious belief, genes or fingerprints.	Personal data, revealing racial or ethnic origin, political opinions, religious or philosophical beliefs, trade-union membership; data concerning health or sex life and sexual orientation; genetic data or biometric data.
Breach Notification Requirements	The Guideline recommends that Data Administrators should promptly notify a data breach to affected data subjects, and in case of major breach promptly report to the personal information protection management department. Under the Cybersecurity Law, network operators must promptly inform data subjects if their personal information is disclosed, tampered with or destroyed, and notification must also be made promptly to the relevant authorities.	In the event of a data breach, the controller must report the breach to the DPA without undue delay, and in any event within 72 hours of becoming aware of it. There is an exception where the data breach is unlikely to result in any harm to data subjects.
Data Disposal Requirements	None	Personal information can be retained only as long as necessary for the disclosed purposes.
Data Controller and Processor Registration Requirements	Chinese law does not require controllers and processors to register with government authorities.	There is no registration requirement however a data collector or processor must consult with the DPA if processing would result in a high risk in the absence of measures taken by a data controller to mitigate the risk.
Data Protection Officer Requirements	None	A controller or processor must appoint a DPO if local laws require it to do so, or if its data processing activities involve: regular and systematic monitoring of data subjects on a large scale; or processing Sensitive Personal Data on a large scale.
Access, Rectification,	Under the Guideline, a data collector or processor must allow a subject a	A data collector or processor allow a subject a right of access to

and Deletion Requirements	right of access to personal information held by an organization and a right to correct inaccuracies in or update their personal information records.	personal information held by an organization and a right to correct inaccuracies in/update their personal information records.
Consent and Notice Requirements	Under the Guideline, consent is required from the data subject before the personal information can be processed. Consent can be explicit or implicit. Implicit consent is sufficient for collection of general personal information. Explicit consent is required for collection of sensitive personal information.	Consent must be freely given, specific, informed and unambiguous indication of his or her wishes by which the data subject, either by a statement or by a clear affirmative action, signifies agreement to personal data relating to them being processed.

Country	Germany	India
Regulatory and Enforcement Agency/Privacy Laws	Each German state has a Data Protection Authority which is responsible for the enforcement of data protection laws. Federal Data Protection Act (Bundesdatenschutzgesetz) (BDSG) Additionally, each German state has its own data protection law. The data protection acts of the individual states protect personal data from processing and use by public authorities whereas the BDSG protects personal data from processing and use by federal public authorities and private bodies. Note: When the European Data Protection Regulation comes into force in 2018. It will completely replace the BDSG.	No centralized enforcement agency. The Information Technology Act, 2000 regulates electronic data and non-electronic records or information that have been, are currently or are intended to be processed electronically. Information Technology (Reasonable Security Practices and Procedures and Sensitive Personal Data or Information) Rules (Privacy Rules) regulate corporate who engage in collecting, processing and storing personal data, including sensitive personal information.
Protected Personal Information Defined	The BDSG defines personal data as any information concerning the personal or material circumstances of an identified or identifiable natural person (data subject).	Any information that relates to a natural person, which either directly or indirectly, in combination with other information that is available or likely to be available to a corporate entity, is capable of identifying such person.
Sensitive Information Defined	The BDSG defines sensitive data as any information on racial or ethnic origin, political opinions, religious or	Information relating to: • password • financial information • health information

	philosophical beliefs, trade union membership, health or sex life.	• sexual orientation • biometric information
Breach Notification Requirements	The BDSG contains a breach notification duty which applies if: sensitive personal data, personal data subject to professional secrecy, personal data related to criminal and/or administrative offences, personal data concerning bank or credit card accounts, certain telecommunications and online data is abused or lost and an unauthorized third party acquires knowledge of said data. An organization should notify their relevant data protection authority and the data subjects effected.	In the event of a breach an organization should notify the Indian Computer Emergency Response Team (Cert-In) within a reasonable amount of time.
Data Disposal Requirements	Personal information can be retained only if it necessary for the disclosed purposes.	Personal information can be retained only if necessary for the disclosed purposes.
Data Controller and Processor Registration Requirements	Private organizations must, register with the relevant supervisory authorities. Unless the data controller has appointed a data, protection officer and has no more than nine employees and consent has been obtained from the data subjects or the collection, processing or use is needed to create, carry out or terminate a legal obligation or quasi-legal obligation with the data subjects.	Indian law does not require controllers and processors to register with government authorities.
Data Protection Officer Requirements	Data controllers that deploy more than nine persons in relation to the automated processing of personal data are obliged to appoint a DPO.	Every corporate entity collecting sensitive personal information, rather than, personal must appoint a DPO.
Access, Rectification, and Deletion Requirements	Under the BDSG a data collector or processor must allow a subject a right of access to personal information held by an organization and a right to correct inaccuracies in or update their personal information records.	An organization must, on request by an individual, give that individual access to the personal information (and the ability to correct inaccurate information.
Consent and Notice Requirements	The collection, processing and use of personal data is only admissible if explicitly permitted by the BDSG or any other legal provision or if the data subject has explicitly consented in advance.	Any corporate entity or any person acting on its behalf, collecting sensitive personal information, must obtain written consent from a data subject.

Country	Japan	Netherlands
Regulatory and Enforcement Agency/Privacy Laws	Privacy Protection Commission (the "Commission") The Act on the Protection of Personal Information ("APPI") requires business operators who utilize for their business in Japan a personal information database which consists of more than 5,000 individuals in total identified by personal information on any day in the past six months to protect personal information. Amendments to the APPI, which were passed in 2015 and go into effect no later than September 2017[1] (the "Amendments"), apply the APPI to all businesses in Japan, regardless of whether the business operator maintains a database of more than 5,000 individuals.	Dutch Data Protection Authority (Autoriteit Persoonsgegevens). Dutch Personal Data Protection Act (Wbp) regulates the collection and processing of personal data or sensitive personal data. When European Data Protection Regulation comes into force in 2018. The Data Protection Regulation will then completely replace the Wbp.
Protected Personal Information Defined	Information about a living individual which can identify the specific individual by name, date of birth or other description contained in such information.	Any data relating to an identified or identifiable natural person.
Sensitive Information Defined	Information about a person's race, creed, social status, medical history, criminal record, any crimes a person has been a victim of, and any other information that might cause the person to be discriminated against.	Personal data regarding a person's religion or philosophy of life, race, political persuasion, health and sexual life, trade union membership, criminal behavior and personal data regarding unlawful or objectionable conduct connected with a ban imposed as a result of such conduct.
Breach Notification Requirements	The APPI does not explicitly require notification to a ministry or governmental authority in the event of a leak or security breach that may lead to a leak of personal data, although a ministry may request that a report be submitted on a voluntary basis. The guidelines on this point are under preparation.	A data breach must be reported to the Autoriteit Persoonsgegevens and the data subject, if such data breach has or may have serious disadvantageous consequences for the protection of personal data.
Data Disposal Requirements	Personal information can be retained only as long as necessary for the disclosed purposes.	Personal information can be retained only as long as necessary for the disclosed purposes.

Data Controller and Processor Registration Requirements	Japanese law does not require controllers and processors to register with government authorities.	Data controllers who process personal data by automatic means must register with the Autoriteit Persoonsgegevens.
Data Protection Officer Requirements	None	None
Access, Rectification, and Deletion Requirements	An organization must, on request by an individual, give that individual access to the personal information (and the ability to correct inaccurate information.	An organization must, on request by an individual, give that individual access to the personal information (and the ability to correct inaccurate information.
Consent and Notice Requirements	Organizations must obtain free, informed and express consent of a data subject for the collection, use, storage, transfer and treatment of personal data online.	Organizations must obtain free, informed and express consent of a data subject for the collection, use, storage, transfer and treatment of personal data online.

Country	Russia	South Africa
Regulatory and Enforcement Agency/Privacy Laws	Federal Service for Supervision of Communications, Information Technologies and Mass Media (Roscomnadzor) Data Protection Act No. 152 FZ (DPA) regulates personal data collection processing and storage.	The Information Regulator Protection of Personal Information Act ("POPI"), regulates the processing of personal information by public and private bodies.
Protected Personal Information Defined	Any data relating to an identified or identifiable natural person. Personal data is defined in law as any information that relates directly or indirectly to the specific or defined physical person (the data subject). This can be widely interpreted in various contexts, so it is important to consider each situation carefully.	Information relating to an identifiable, living, natural person including: information relating to the race, gender, sex, pregnancy, marital status, national, ethnic or social origin; color, sexual orientation, age, physical or mental health, well-being, disability, religion, conscience, belief; culture, language and birth of the person; information relating to the education, medical, financial, criminal or employment history of the person; any identifying number, symbol, e-mail address, physical address, telephone number, location information, online identifier or other particular assignment to the person; the biometric information of the person; the personal opinions,

		views or preferences of the person; correspondence sent by the person that is implicitly or explicitly of a private or confidential nature or further correspondence that would reveal the contents of the original correspondence; the views or opinions of another individual about the person; and the name of the person if it appears with other personal information relating to the person or if the disclosure of the name itself would reveal information about the person.
Sensitive Information Defined	Sensitive personal data is defined as special categories of personal data in Russian legislation. Such special categories include data related to race, national identity, political opinions, religious and philosophical beliefs, health state, intimacies and biometrical data.	Information concerning religious or philosophical beliefs, race or ethnic origin, trade union membership, political persuasion, health or sex life or biometric information or criminal behavior (to the extent that such information relates to the alleged commission of an offence or any proceedings in respect of any offence allegedly committed, or the disposal of such proceedings).
Breach Notification Requirements	There is no mandatory requirement to report data security breaches or losses to the Agency or to data subjects.	A data breach must be reported to the Information Regulator and the data subject as soon as possible unless the identity of such data subject cannot be established.
Data Disposal Requirements	Personal information can be retained only as long as necessary for the disclosed purposes.	Personal information can be retained only as long as necessary for the disclosed purposes.
Data Controller and Processor Registration Requirements	Russian requires controllers and processors to register with the Roscomnadzor.	DPOs must be registered with the Information Regulator.
Data Protection Officer Requirements	Every legal entity collecting personal information, must appoint a DPO.	Every legal entity collecting personal information, must appoint a DPO.
Access, Rectification, and Deletion Requirements	An organization must, on request by an individual, give that individual access to the personal information (and the ability to correct inaccurate information.	An organization must, on request by an individual, give that individual access to the personal information (and the ability to correct inaccurate information.

Consent and Notice Requirements	Organizations must obtain free, informed and express consent of a data subject for the collection, use, storage, transfer and treatment of personal data online.	Organizations must obtain free, informed and express consent of a data subject for the collection, use, storage, transfer and treatment of personal data online.

Country	**United Kingdom**	**United States**
Regulatory and Enforcement Agency/Privacy Laws	Information Commissioner's Office (ICO) Data Protection Act 1998 (DPA) regulates the collection and processing of personal data. When European Data Protection Regulation comes into force in 2018. The Data Protection Regulation will then completely replace the DPA. It is anticipated the process of Brexit will not impact this transition.	There is no single data protection authority in the United States. However, the Federal Trade Commission (FTC) can issue and enforce privacy regulations. There is no federal single privacy law in the United States; however there are a number federal and state sectoral laws that address privacy.
Protected Personal Information Defined	Data relating to living individuals who can be identified from the data, or any expression of opinion about the individual.	Varies widely by regulation however it can deduced as information that on its own or combination with other data actually identify a person.
Sensitive Information Defined	Data consisting of information as to: • the racial or ethnic origin of the data subject • his political opinions • his religious beliefs or other beliefs of a similar nature • whether he is a member of a trade union • his physical or mental health or condition • his sexual life • the commission or alleged commission by him of any offence, or • any proceedings for any offence committed or alleged to have been committed by him, the disposal of such proceedings or the sentence of any court in such proceedings.	Varies widely by sector however the Department of Homeland Security provides a general definition which states: ""Personally Identifiable Information, which if lost, compromised, or disclosed without authorization, could result in substantial harm, embarrassment, inconvenience, or unfairness to an individual."
Breach Notification Requirements	There is no mandatory requirement in the Act to report data security breaches or losses to the ICO unless "a large number of people are affected" or the consequences of the	Breach notification requirements vary by sector as there is not an overriding federal privacy law. 48 US states, Washington, D.C. and most US territories (including,

	breach are particularly "serious", the ICO should be informed.	Puerto Rico, Guam and the Virgin Islands) require notifying state residents of a security breach.
Data Disposal Requirements	Personal information can be retained only as long as necessary for the disclosed purposes.	Personal information can be retained only as long as necessary for the disclosed purposes
Data Controller and Processor Registration Requirements	Data controllers who process personal data must inform the Information Commissioner.	None
Data Protection Officer Requirements	None	Only the federal health information privacy law, HIPAA, requires an organization to appoint a data protection officer.
Access, Rectification, and Deletion Requirements	An organization must, on request by an individual, give that individual access to the personal information (and the ability to correct inaccurate information.	As a general rule most law regulating data privacy require that an organization must, on request by an individual, give that individual access to the personal information (and the ability to correct inaccurate information.
Consent and Notice Requirements	Organizations must obtain free, informed and express consent of a data subject for the collection, use, storage, transfer and treatment of personal data online.	As a general rule most law regulating data privacy require that organizations must obtain free, informed and express consent of a data subject for the collection, use, storage, transfer and treatment of personal data online.

95027801R00085

Made in the USA
Columbia, SC
03 May 2018